# CORPORATE GOVERNANCE: IMPROVING COMPETITIVENESS AND ACCESS TO CAPITAL IN GLOBAL MARKETS

## A REPORT TO THE OECD
## BY THE BUSINESS SECTOR ADVISORY GROUP
## ON CORPORATE GOVERNANCE

ORGANISATION FOR ECONOMIC CO-OPERATION AND DEVELOPMENT

# ORGANISATION FOR ECONOMIC CO-OPERATION AND DEVELOPMENT

Pursuant to Article 1 of the Convention signed in Paris on 14th December 1960, and which came into force on 30th September 1961, the Organisation for Economic Co-operation and Development (OECD) shall promote policies designed:

- to achieve the highest sustainable economic growth and employment and a rising standard of living in Member countries, while maintaining financial stability, and thus to contribute to the development of the world economy;
- to contribute to sound economic expansion in Member as well as non-member countries in the process of economic development; and
- to contribute to the expansion of world trade on a multilateral, non-discriminatory basis in accordance with international obligations.

The original Member countries of the OECD are Austria, Belgium, Canada, Denmark, France, Germany, Greece, Iceland, Ireland, Italy, Luxembourg, the Netherlands, Norway, Portugal, Spain, Sweden, Switzerland, Turkey, the United Kingdom and the United States. The following countries became Members subsequently through accession at the dates indicated hereafter: Japan (28th April 1964), Finland (28th January 1969), Australia (7th June 1971), New Zealand (29th May 1973), Mexico (18th May 1994), the Czech Republic (21st December 1995), Hungary (7th May 1996), Poland (22nd November 1996) and Korea (12th December 1996). The Commission of the European Communities takes part in the work of the OECD (Article 13 of the OECD Convention).

Publié en français sous le titre :

LE GOUVERNEMENT D'ENTREPRISE : AMÉLIORER LA COMPÉTITIVITÉ DES ENTREPRISES ET FACILITER LEUR ACCÈS AUX MARCHÉS FINANCIERS MONDIAUX
Rapport à l'OCDE du Groupe consultatif du secteur privé sur le gouvernement d'entreprise

Reprinted 1998

# TABLE OF CONTENTS

# LETTER FROM THE CHAIRMAN

2 April 1998

Dear Mr. Secretary-General,

I am pleased to submit to the OECD the Report of the Business Sector Advisory Group on Corporate Governance, entitled "Corporate Governance: Improving Competitiveness and Access to Capital in Global Markets".

OECD economies increasingly rely on the vitality and strength of their respective private sectors, in what has become a world market. The corporation is the primary engine of each respective private sector – it raises capital, creates jobs, earns profit, and divides its value added among those contributing to its success.

The governance of the corporation, the internal means by which it accomplishes its performance, is therefore of current great international interest and concern. There is little debate that good corporate governance can positively impact the corporation's overall economic performance. Moreover, there is little debate that transparent corporate governance is key to accessing global capital markets; visible governance provides investors with a definitive description of their rights *vis à vis* the corporation.

While governance is comprised of the internal relationships amongst shareholders, boards of directors, and managers, those relationships are the result of government regulations, public perception and voluntary private initiatives. To understand those relationships requires an understanding of the respective roles of the government and private sector in shaping corporate governance.

Recognising the significance of corporate governance to the economies of its Member countries, and the necessary interplay of governmental and private sector initiatives involved, the OECD determined to ascertain whether it could be of significant assistance to its Members in developing an understanding of the respective roles of government and private sector. Such an understanding would be of invaluable assistance to policy makers, public and private, throughout the OECD Member countries.

At the 1996 meeting of the Council at Ministerial level, OECD Ministers requested that there be commenced such a study of corporate governance. The Business Sector Advisory Group on Corporate Governance was established that same year to review and analyse international corporate governance issues and to suggest an agenda and priorities for further OECD initiatives.

Since that time, the Advisory Group has met in Paris on a number of occasions and, between meetings, has communicated in writing and through telephone conferences. As an integral part of its work, the Advisory Group has consulted with a wide circle of business sector practitioners from OECD Member countries and has held a Business Sector Colloquium on Corporate Governance in June 1997 to achieve even greater input. A summary of the Colloquium discussions, and a list of participants and other commentators is appended to this Report. The quotations in the text of this Report derive from this Colloquium.

In addition, the Advisory Group has invited and received comments on the Colloquium topics including comments through BIAC (the Business and Industry Advisory Committee to the OECD) and comments submitted by Australian business leaders who participated in a series of related colloquia sponsored by the Australian Institute of Company Directors, Blake Dawson Waldron Lawyers and the Australian Stock Exchange Limited.

All of this input has provided a rich resource base for the Advisory Group to draw on in formulating its Report, and has assisted the Group to identify some key areas of common understanding:

◊ Corporate governance practices constantly evolve to meet changing conditions. As a work-in-progress, there is no single universal model of corporate governance. Nor is there a static, final structure in corporate governance that every country or corporation should emulate. Experimentation and variety should be expected and encouraged.

◊ Corporate governance practices vary and will continue to vary across nations and cultures. We can learn a great deal from observing experiences in other countries.

◊ Corporate governance practices will also vary as a function of ownership structures, business circumstances, competitive conditions, corporate life cycle and numerous other factors.

There are, however, a few fundamental parameters:

◊ Increasingly, it is accepted that the corporate objective is maximising shareholder value, which not only requires superior competitive performance but also generally requires responsiveness to the demands and expectations of other stakeholders.

◊ Increased transparency and independent oversight of management by boards of directors are the central elements of improved corporate governance.

◊ Board practice should be subject to voluntary adaptation and evolution, in an environment of globally understood minimum standards.

◊ There are certain areas in which the adoption of universal rules is preferable (such as in accounting).

The Advisory Group has endeavored in this Report to explain why it has emphasized the foregoing parameters as a basis for both public and private sector initiatives to improve corporate governance throughout the OECD countries, to suggest certain public and private initiatives and to suggest an agenda and priorities for further OECD efforts in corporate governance.

We hope therefore that this Report will contribute positively to the economic performance of corporations throughout the OECD countries, and thereby contribute to the welfare and prosperity of their respective economies and citizens.

It has been a great honour, as well as an intellectual and personal pleasure, to chair the Advisory Group and work with its highly talented and experienced members – Michel Albert, Sir Adrian Cadbury, Robert E. Denham, Dieter Feddersen and Nobuo Tateisi. Each Advisory Group member has contributed generously of his time and insights – all in his individual capacity, and not as representatives of any organisation, government or country. I think

9

the Report reflects this remarkable collaboration, which enabled a consensus to emerge from individuals grounded in diverse national and cultural experiences.

The Advisory Group wishes to emphasize that this Report reflects the consensus of the Advisory Group members as regards the principal perspectives and recommendations set forth. Individual members may not necessarily agree with every aspect of the Report.

On behalf of the Advisory Group, I wish to thank Joanna R. Shelton, Deputy Secretary-General of the OECD, for her considerable intellectual support and assistance. We especially wish to acknowledge the substantive research, drafting and organisational assistance of Mats Isaksson and Rauf Gönenç of the OECD staff. They were instrumental in organising the June 1997 Colloquium, and in providing each of the members of the Advisory Group, and certainly its Chairman, with knowledgeable and steady assistance throughout. Thanks also to Holly J. Gregory of Weil, Gotshal & Manges LLP, for her invaluable editing of this Report, and her assistance in co-ordinating much of the communications on which this Report is based.

Finally, on behalf of the Advisory Group, I thank you and the OECD for the opportunity to explore and comment on the important issues of corporate governance in the context of evolving international markets.

Sincerely yours,

Ira M. Millstein
Chairman

# MEMBERS OF THE OECD BUSINESS SECTOR ADVISORY GROUP ON CORPORATE GOVERNANCE

**Mr. Ira M. Millstein** (Chairman), Senior Partner, Weil, Gotshal & Manges LLP; Eugene F. Williams, Jr. Visiting Professor in Competitive Enterprise and Strategy at the Yale School of Management; Chairman of the National Association of Corporate Directors Commission on Director Professionalism; Member, American Academy of Arts and Sciences; author of *The Limits of Corporate Power* and various articles on governance topics. United States.

**Mr. Michel Albert,** Member of the Monetary Policy Council, Banque de France, Former Chairman, Assurances Générales de France (AGF); author of several books on social and economic matters, including *Capitalism versus Capitalism.* France.

**Sir Adrian Cadbury,** Former Chairman, Cadbury-Schweppes; Chairman, Committee on the Financial Aspects of Corporate Governance 1991-95; contributor to several works in the area of corporate governance and author of *The Company Chairman.* United Kingdom.

**Mr. Robert E. Denham,** Former Chairman and Chief Executive Officer, Salomon Inc. (parent company of Salomon Brothers); Member, Independence Standards Board (rule-making body for auditor independence); Member, Board of Trustees, The Conference Board; Member, President's Bipartisan Commission on Entitlement and Tax Reform. United States.

**Prof. Dr. Dieter Feddersen,** Partner, Feddersen Laule Scherzberg & Ohle Hansen Ewerwahn; Honorary Professor, University of Heidelberg; Chairman and member of several Supervisory Boards in German Aktiengesellschaften and GmbHs; Member, German American Lawyers Association, International Fiscal Association and several other learned and non-profit organisations. Germany.

**Mr. Nobuo Tateisi,** Chairman and Representative Director, OMRON Corporation; Vice Chairman, Policy Board Member, Chairman of ILO Committee and Chairman of the International Committee of the Japan Federation of Employers' Association (Nikkeiren); Co-Chairman of the Committee on Asia and Oceania of the Japan Federation of Economic Organization (Keidanren); Vice Chairman of the Council for Better Corporate Citizenship (CBCC); and Vice Chairman of the Japan Institute for Social and Economic Affairs (Keizai Koho Center). Japan.

# SECRETARIAT

Mr. Rauf Gönenç
Principal Administrator
Industry Division
OECD

Mr. Mats Isaksson
Principal Administrator
Industry Division
OECD

Ms. Holly J. Gregory
Counsel
Weil, Gotshal & Manges LLP
New York

# CHAPTER 1. OVERVIEW, PUBLIC POLICY PERSPECTIVES AND RECOMMENDATIONS TO THE OECD

## 1.1 Corporate Governance in a New Economic Environment

1. Individual OECD nations are at an economic (and perhaps social) watershed as their market-oriented economies increasingly rely on the vitality and strength of the private sector in what rapidly is becoming a world market. OECD economies rely on the corporation – as the engine, worldwide, for private sector participation in the global market – to raise capital, create jobs, earn profits and divide the value added among those contributing to its success.

2. To succeed in their primary objective of generating long-term economic profit, corporations must seek to achieve a sustained competitive advantage. This requires significant flexibility to take necessary risks in responding quickly to opportunities and challenges in a constantly changing environment. Corporations must be able to develop and implement their respective competitive advantages, to raise capital, to assemble and redeploy resources to that end and, at the same time, to meet the expectations of their shareholders, employees, suppliers, creditors, customers, communities and society at large.

3. Corporate governance comprehends that structure of relationships and corresponding responsibilities among a core group consisting of shareholders, board members and managers designed to best foster the competitive performance required to achieve the corporation's primary objective.

4. Corporate governance tends to gain public attention when performance problems are apparent, both at national and company levels. For example, the current crisis in East Asian economies is generating considerable discussion about failed corporate governance practices relating to lending and borrowing. Similarly, performance problems at the company level frequently draw attention to governance problems. While developing appropriate remedies for cases of visible failure is important, the more long-term policy objective is

to prevent such failures. All OECD nations share this challenge in their efforts to improve the functioning of their market economies.

5.     While there may be some debate in the academic literature about the impact of corporate governance on corporate performance, the Advisory Group is convinced – based on its collective experience, the views of respected business groups, and recent research and academic commentary – that improved corporate governance can positively impact overall corporate performance.

6.     The quality of corporate governance is of particular importance at a time when interactions between corporations and their capital suppliers are undergoing fundamental changes, with significant implications for other corporate stakeholders, such as employees. Given the globalisation of competition in markets for goods, services, key human resources and capital, corporations in all OECD countries face common competitive challenges and opportunities. Due to global deregulation and technological change, capital suppliers are encountering new opportunities to improve their returns; entrepreneurs and companies are exposed to a wider and more complete range of capital-raising vehicles; and employees are experiencing greater exposure to the risks and rewards of increased competition.

7.     With international deregulation, investment capital is more mobile and investors are demanding broader investment opportunities with internationally competitive levels of profitability (risk-adjusted returns). For corporations, this development has brought about access to a wider pool of financing and a greater range of risk- and reward-sharing equity placements; broader financing options in turn can support a variety of research and development activities, spin-offs, capacity expansion and new firm creation. However, greater competition for capital results in greater pressure for corporate economic performance and significant pressures on long-standing relationships with employees.

> *"Due to domestic and international deregulation, financial institutions have access to a much broader group of investment opportunities, which has resulted in very aggressive return expectations. Enhanced opportunities to find higher returns on investments have raised a challenge for all companies competing to attract capital."*
>
> Ms. Heidi Kunz, Chief Financial Officer, ITT Industries (United States)

8.      Good corporate governance should allow corporations and economies to capture fully the inherent benefits from these developments while maintaining a sensitivity to the social concerns raised. Failure to adapt to efficient governance practices may well lead to restricted access to capital markets. Again, the current crisis in East Asian economies provides a stark example. Capital providers increasingly rely on the corporate governance of the corporations they invest in, or lend to, to provide actual accountability and responsibility to investors and lenders.

9.      Because worldwide the corporation is the essential engine driving the private sector economically, and because corporate governance can be critical to competitive performance in all of a corporation's markets (goods, services, capital and human resources), the quality of corporate governance can affect the dynamism of the private sector and ultimately the credibility of market economies in providing economic growth and promoting citizen welfare. Accordingly, corporate governance has become an important international topic for discussion.

10.     The task of adapting, refining and adjusting corporate governance is a necessary and ongoing process. To be competitive, both corporations and investors must be allowed to innovate relentlessly and to adapt their governance practices to new economic circumstances; corporate governance should be viewed as "work in progress". For this reason, the Advisory Group rejects a "one-size-fits-all" approach to corporate governance practice and focuses this Report on a set of general public policy perspectives and guiding norms in a context of pluralism and adaptability.

11.     To enable flexibility, experimentation and continuous improvement, the design of corporate governance relationships and practices should be left to market forces: corporate governance should remain, basically, decisions by individual actors in the private sector. While the need to protect investor rights is undisputed, the Advisory Group believes that market-driven solutions emerging from competition among alternative practices are generally superior to those mandated by regulating authorities.

12.     This market-based perspective does not exclude a role for government. Policy makers and regulatory bodies have a distinct and important responsibility for shaping a regulatory framework, compatible with their respective societal values, that allows market forces to work and permits investors and companies to design their governance arrangements in accordance with their respective needs.

13. The collective efforts of the business community to evaluate and disseminate experiences in the form of "best practices" and governance guidelines are important as well. It is the Advisory Group's view that such efforts increase the collective knowledge about workable solutions and thereby help to invigorate a broad understanding of the principles underlying good corporate governance practices, and the continued evolution of better practices.

14. Although this Report focuses on publicly traded corporations (*i.e.* corporations whose stock is listed on a stock exchange or other market), the Advisory Group believes that many of the issues discussed are also of importance to wholly privately held, family-owned and state-owned companies – which account for a significant portion of economic activity in many OECD countries. Increasingly, banks and other lenders are relying on principles of improved corporate governance to protect their investments. Moreover, privately held, family-owned and state-owned companies are affected by corporate governance standards as soon as they seek capital from equity markets to finance their activities (and convert into the legal structure of a publicly traded corporation). Therefore, privately held, family-owned and state-owned companies – many of which will be the publicly traded companies of tomorrow – are well-advised to consider the corporate governance principles applicable to publicly traded corporations.

## 1.2    An Agenda for Modernisation

15. The Advisory Group believes that enabling the corporation to improve its competitiveness and access to capital markets through improved corporate governance will require both public policy and private sector initiatives. The Advisory Group offers this Report to promote supportive international public policy perspectives, to encourage voluntary private sector initiatives and, particularly, to offer the OECD suggestions about the direction of its further efforts.

---

*"There will be increased pressure on all our economies and societies to adjust to the requirements of global financial markets. This process of convergence must of course be guided by building up a consensus on what should be the rules of the game. Institutions like the OECD can play an important role in shaping that process."*

Dr. Henning Schulte-Noelle, Chairman of the Board of Management, Allianz AG (Germany)

---

16.    The Advisory Group suggests that such further public and private sector initiatives – and OECD efforts – focus on the following Agenda (which is described in the remaining chapters of this Report):

◊ *Defining the mission of the corporation in the modern economy:* Generating long-term economic gain to enhance shareholder (or investor) value is necessary to attract equity investment capital and is, therefore, the corporation's central mission. At the same time, however, corporations must function in the larger society. To varying degrees, different national systems and individual corporations may temper the economic objective of the corporation to address non-economic objectives. Full transparency of economic and non-economic objectives – both as to the national system and the individual corporation – will be necessary in the global competition for capital. (Chapter 2)

◊ *Ensuring adaptability of corporate governance arrangements:* The primary role for regulation is to shape a corporate governance environment, compatible with societal values, that allows competition and market forces to work so that corporations can succeed in generating long-term economic gain. Specific governance structures or practices will not necessarily fit all companies at all times. Nor should it be taken for granted that a given design may suit the same company during different stages of its development. For dynamic enterprises operating in a rapidly changing world, corporate governance adaptability and flexibility – supported by an enabling regulatory framework – is a prerequisite for better corporate performance. (Chapter 3)

◊ *Protecting shareholder rights:* For companies to attract equity investment, regulatory safeguards must emphasize fairness, transparency and accountability. These safeguards should take into account the new and growing category of non-controlling shareholders who have emerged in the form of institutional investors. The focus of current efforts to improve shareholder protection should centre on investor access to performance-related information, shareholder exercise of voting rights, and promotion of active and independent (non-executive) members of boards of directors to strengthen the quality of corporate governance. (Chapter 4)

17

◊ *Enabling active investing:* Active owners can play a distinct role in strengthening a corporation's ability to exploit new business opportunities. Such active investment should be encouraged, but with adequate protections for more passive holders. (Chapter 5)

◊ *Aligning the interests of shareholders and other stakeholders:* Corporate success is linked to the ability to align the interests of directors, managers and employees with the interests of shareholders. Performance-based compensation is a useful tool for this purpose. Independent (non-executive) members of the board of directors – or in certain nations, board of auditors – have a special responsibility in designing and approving appropriate remuneration schemes. (Chapter 6)

◊ *Recognising societal interests:* Companies do not act independently from the societies in which they operate. Accordingly, corporate actions must be compatible with societal objectives concerning social cohesion, individual welfare and equal opportunities for all. Attending to legitimate social concerns should, in the long run, benefit all parties, including investors. At times, however, there may be a trade-off between short-term social costs and the long-term benefits to society of having a healthy, competitive private sector. Societal needs that transcend the responsive ability of the private sector should be met by specific public policy measures, rather than by impeding improvements in corporate governance and capital allocation. (Chapter 7)

17.    The specific topics on this Agenda are interrelated and comple-mentary. Therefore, the consequences of any particular public policy reform measure need to be carefully considered to ensure a coherent approach to corporate governance.

18.    Based on its discussion of this Agenda in the ensuing Chapters, the Advisory Group has formulated Perspectives that it believes should guide:

◊ public policy makers and regulators to encourage the development of improved governance practices, with strong emphasis on government enabling voluntary private sector development rather than attempting to regulate it; and

◊ corporations and investors voluntarily to improve governance practices.

19.    Based on these Perspectives, and the Advisory Group's discussion of specific substantive issues in this Report, the Advisory Group has also formulated Recommendations for further efforts by the OECD.

### 1.3    Perspectives for Public Policy Improvement

20.    For the private sector and specifically the publicly traded corporation to flourish, policy makers and regulators need to shape a corporate governance environment, compatible with the respective society's values, that allows market forces to work and corporations to succeed in generating long-term economic profit. Largely this entails protecting the integrity and efficiency of capital markets (thus promoting confidence), by protecting shareholder rights and providing for the disclosure of information.

21.    Since regulation is a powerful and potentially rigid tool, it should be used with care in the context of corporate governance. If corporations are to fulfill their potential in exploiting opportunities to create long-term economic profit, market forces must be allowed to determine the most efficient deployment of investment and other corporate resources.

22.    Protecting shareholders and promoting investor confidence are key elements in providing the access to capital needed to create and maintain a dynamic, competitive corporate sector. By focusing primarily on shareholder protection, disclosure of information and voluntary corporate governance improvements, policy makers and regulators can avoid developing overly rigid and intrusive regulatory systems.

*Perspective 1 (Flexibility). Policy makers and regulators should be sensitive to corporations' need for flexibility in responding to the changing competitive environment and the related need for flexible, adaptive governance structures. Regulation should support a range of ownership and governance forms so that a market for governance arrangements develops.*

*Perspective 2 (Regulatory Impact). Policy makers and regulators should consider the impact of any proposed regulatory initiative on the ability of the corporate sector to respond to competitive market environments. They should avoid those regulations that threaten to unduly interfere with market mechanisms.*

◊ *The Advisory Group endorses and encourages efforts by the OECD to promote greater reliance on competition and market forces through its multi-sector study of regulatory reform. The Advisory Group invites the international business community to support the OECD's efforts.*

**Perspective 3 (Regulatory Focus).** *Regulatory intervention in the area of corporate governance is likely to be most effective if limited to:*

◊ *Ensuring the protection of shareholder rights and the enforceability of contracts with resource providers (Fairness);*

◊ *Requiring timely disclosure of adequate information concerning corporate financial performance (Transparency);*

◊ *Clarifying governance roles and responsibilities, and supporting voluntary efforts to ensure the alignment of managerial and shareholder interests, as monitored by boards of directors – or in certain nations, boards of auditors – having some independent members (Accountability); and*

◊ *Ensuring corporate compliance with the other laws and regulations that reflect the respective society's values (Responsibility).*

### 1.3.1 Fairness

23. To encourage both the domestic and foreign capital investment necessary for the development of globally competitive enterprises, shareholders require reasonable assurances that their assets will be protected against fraud, managerial or controlling shareholder self-dealing, and other "insider" wrongdoing.

24. Market confidence also depends on a clear understanding of – and faith in – contractual relationships among other corporate resource providers and consumers, and an expectation that contractual relationships are enforceable.

**Perspective 4 (Clarity, Consistency, Enforceability).** *Policy makers and regulators should provide clear, consistent and enforceable securities and capital market regulations designed to protect shareholder rights and create legal systems capable of enforcing such regulations. Such regulations should seek to treat all equity investors – including minority shareholders – fairly, and should include protections against fraud, dilution, self-dealing and insider trading.*

*Perspective 5 (Litigation Abuse).* Regulations aimed at protecting shareholder rights should be designed to protect against litigation abuse. This can be accomplished through the use of tests for the sufficiency of shareholder complaints and the provision of safe harbours for management and director actions.

*Perspective 6 (Basic Contract, Commercial and Consumer Law).* Policy makers and regulators should ensure that an adequate system of contract, commercial and basic consumer protection law is in place, so that contractual relationships are enforceable. (This is particularly relevant to those developing and emerging market nations with less established legal systems.)

*Perspective 7 (Regulatory Impact on Active Investors).* Policy makers and regulators should review whether their securities, tax and other regulations unduly hinder active investors, and whether their regulations concerning institutional investors inappropriately inhibit them from participating as active investors.

*Perspective 8 (Corruption and Bribery).* Policy makers and regulators should ensure that corporations function in an environment that is free from corruption and bribery.

◊ *The Advisory Group welcomes the OECD Convention on Combating Bribery of Foreign Public Officials in International Business Transactions and encourages efforts by the OECD to establish common international rules outlawing bribery by corporations. The Advisory Group invites the international business community to support the OECD's efforts.*

### 1.3.2    Transparency

25.    Investor confidence and market efficiency depend on the disclosure of accurate, timely information about corporate performance. To be of value in the global capital markets, disclosed information should be clear, consistent and comparable. This enables investors worldwide to make educated decisions concerning the allocation of their assets, and provides high-performing corporations with lower-cost capital.

*Perspective 9 (Accurate, Timely Disclosure).* Regulators should require that corporations disclose accurate, timely information concerning corporate financial performance. Adequate enforcement mechanisms should be provided.

***Perspective 10 (Consistent, Comparable Disclosure).*** *Regulators should co-operate internationally in developing clear, consistent and comparable standards for disclosure of corporate financial performance, including accounting standards.*

***Perspective 11 (Ownership Disclosure).*** *Regulators should extend such disclosure requirements to the corporate ownership structure, including disclosure of any special voting rights and of the beneficial ownership of controlling or major blocks of shares.*

***Perspective 12 (Disclosure Improvement).*** *Regulators should encourage ongoing improvements in both disclosure techniques and formats. This may encompass both the use of new information technologies, and the disclosure of non-financial but relevant information concerning intangible assets.*

### 1.3.3   Accountability

26.      The potential for management and shareholder interests to diverge is a defining characteristic of the modern, publicly traded corporation. Addressing this "agency" problem is a central concern of corporate governance, and the system of rights and responsibilities it encompasses. For corporate governance to be most effective, the major participants – shareholders, directors and managers – need a clear understanding of their respective roles, rights and responsibilities.

27.      The board of directors – or in certain nations, the board of auditors – is uniquely positioned as the internal corporate mechanism for holding management accountable to shareholders. Board oversight can be viewed as a means of reducing the potential for significant divergences between management and investor interests. The board is best positioned to perform this role when – at least to an effective degree – its members are distinct from, and independent of, management. Although the structure of corporate boards for publicly traded corporations differs among OECD nations – for example, by including both single- and two-tier boards – board independence can be promoted in any type of board system.

28.      Accountability generally is based on a system of internal checks and balances. In the corporate context, these include sound audit practices.

29.     Within the broad limits set in a given national economy, each corporation needs flexibility to determine for itself the governance practices that best fit.

*Perspective 13 (Corporate Governance Legal Standards). Policy makers and regulators should articulate clearly the legal standards that govern shareholder, director and management authority and accountability, including their fiduciary roles and legal liabilities. However, because corporate governance and expectations concerning roles and liabilities continue to evolve, legal standards should be flexible and permissive of evolution.*

*Perspective 14 (Shareholder Protection). Policy makers and regulators should protect and enforce shareholders' rights to vote and participate in annual shareholders' meetings.*

*Perspective 15 (Independent Corporate Boards). Policy makers and regulators should encourage some degree of independence in the composition of corporate boards. Stock exchange listing requirements that address a minimal threshold for board independence – and frequently board audit committee independence – have proved useful, while not unduly restrictive or burdensome. However, policy makers and regulators should recognise that corporate governance – including board structure and practice – is not a "one-size-fits-all" proposition, and should be left, largely, to individual participants.*

*Perspective 16 (Sound Audit Practices). Policy makers and regulators should encourage sound audit practices, which include board selection of, and reliance on, an independent auditor.*

*Perspective 17 (Investor Competition). Governments should avoid regulations that unduly inhibit the ability of institutional investors to compete with one another. However, sound, prudent management of these funds should remain the overriding objective of public policy in this area.*

### 1.3.4    Responsibility

30.     While pursuing their objectives, corporations should observe the standards of the societies in which they operate.

31.     In economic systems that rely heavily on market forces to organise the economic foundations of society, a fundamental role of government is to

provide a framework that can support and protect individuals in adjusting to the impacts of market forces.

*Perspective 18 (Law-abiding Corporations). Policy makers and regulators should ensure that corporations abide by laws that uphold the respective society's values, such as criminal, tax, antitrust, labour, environmental protection, equal opportunity, and health and safety laws.*

*Perspective 19 (Individual Welfare). Policy makers and regulators should support and encourage education and training efforts, the provision of unemployment benefits, and other similar efforts aimed at promoting the welfare of individuals.*

*Perspective 20 (Income and Opportunity Divergence). Policy makers and regulators may wish to consider the implications of significant divergence in income and opportunity paths. In particular, government action may be necessary to promote skill acquisition in certain sections of society that do not benefit from present market trends.*

## 1.4    Perspectives for Voluntary Self-improvement

32.    Good corporate governance is a key element in corporate competitiveness and access to capital.

33.    The focal point of corporate governance is the board of directors as a mechanism to represent shareholder interests, prevent conflicts of interest (*i.e.* address the agency problem), monitor managerial performance and balance competing demands on the corporation.

34.    For the board to play this role in a meaningful way, it needs to be capable of acting independently of management. This requires board members (or in some nations, board of auditor members) capable of exercising business judgement independently of management – whether in a single-tier or two-tier board.

35.    Suggested governance "best practices" and individual board guidelines have proliferated in the 1990s and serve as useful tools for board self-improvement.

36.    The right to vote and participate in annual meetings that is generally associated with share ownership is an important investor asset.

*Perspective 21 (Corporate Objective). Individual corporations should disclose the extent to which they pursue projects and policies that diverge from the primary corporate objective of generating long-term economic profit so as to enhance shareholder value in the long term.*

*Perspective 22 (Governance and Competition). Individual corporations and shareholders should recognise the important role that corporate governance plays in positioning the corporation to compete effectively while meeting the expectations of its primary resource providers.*

*Perspective 23 (Board "Best Practices"). Individual corporations, share-holders and other interested parties should continue their efforts to articulate and adopt – voluntarily – corporate governance "best practices" designed to improve board independence and activism, and accountability to shareholders.*

*Perspective 24 (Independent Oversight). Whether in a single-tier or two-tier board system, individual corporations should ensure that an effective number of board of director members – or in certain nations, board of auditor members – are persons who are capable of exercising judgement, independent of management views. Generally, this will require that such board members are persons who are not employed by the company.*

*Perspective 25 (Voting as an Asset). Investors should consider the right to vote and participate in annual meetings as an asset that provides an opportunity to influence the direction and management of the company.*

## 1.5    Recommendations for Further OECD Efforts

37.    The Advisory Group believes that future OECD efforts on corporate governance will be most valuable if they extend beyond collection and synthesis of information about the issues discussed in this Report. OECD efforts should extend to the articulation of a set of common public policy principles to guide national policy reviews and reforms in OECD Member nations, as well as private sector initiatives. The Advisory Group believes that the OECD is ideally situated to formulate a set of common public policy principles, grounded in a review and understanding of Member country governance policies. We expect that such an OECD effort will lead to improved corporate governance, competitiveness and access to capital markets for corporations throughout the world, with resulting benefits to economic growth, employment and society at large.

*Recommendation 1. The Advisory Group recommends that, in its ongoing efforts to encourage Member nations to create an enabling regulatory framework, the OECD pay special attention to the needs of both investors and enterprises in adapting corporate governance arrangements to changing competitive and market forces, so as to support the generation of long-term economic gain and thereby benefit society.*

*Recommendation 2. The Advisory Group recommends that OECD efforts to assist policy reviews in the area of corporate governance be based on the consideration of the Perspectives set forth in this Report, as well as a comparison of OECD nations' corporate governance and disclosure policies and practices, and that such efforts focus on:*

◊ *Formulating and issuing a public policy document or instrument recommending minimum international standards of corporate governance designed to promote fairness, transparency, accountability and responsibility.*

◊ *Formulating and issuing a suggested code of voluntary corporate governance "best practices" designed to improve the board's ability to be responsible and accountable to shareholders, which would encompass processes to ensure board independence.*

◊ *Encouraging common principles for addressing the comparability, reliability and enforcement of corporate disclosure concerning corporate financial performance, corporate ownership structure and corporate governance, culminating in the formulation and issuance of a public policy document or instrument.*

*Recommendation 3. The Advisory Group recommends that, as part of its overall work on corporate governance, the OECD emphasize the importance of societal concerns and the need to clarify responsibilities between the public and private sectors.*

• • •

38.     In the chapters that follow, the Advisory Group discusses the Agenda described above, including the rationales supporting its Perspectives, without restating each such Perspective.

# CHAPTER 2. DEFINING THE MISSION OF THE CORPORATION IN THE MODERN ECONOMY

*Generating long-term economic gain to enhance shareholder (or investor) value is necessary to attract equity investment capital and is, therefore, the corporation's central mission. At the same time, however, corporations must function in the larger society. To varying degrees, different national systems and individual corporations may temper the economic objective of the corporation to address non-economic objectives. Full transparency of economic and non-economic objectives – both as to the national system and the individual corporation – will be necessary in the global competition for capital.*

39.     The Advisory Group recognises that corporations serve a wide variety of economic and social functions, and that responding to competitive pressures in the new environment is likely to influence the content and character of these functions. The Advisory Group believes that, in all OECD economies, the new competitive environment is encouraging a reassessment of traditional corporate governance practices. In some instances, responding to the new competitive environment may require a shift in the corporate objective to focus on the pursuit of economic and social objectives in ways that are sustainable under global product, service and capital market competition.

## 2.1     The Primary Corporate Objective

40.     Most industrialised societies recognise that generating long-term economic profit (a measure based on net revenues that takes into account the cost of capital) is the corporation's primary objective. In the long run, the generation of economic profit to enhance shareholder value, through the pursuit of sustained competitive advantage, is necessary to attract the capital required for prudent growth and perpetuation.

41.     However, "generation of long-term economic profit to enhance shareholder value" is an overly simple description of the task facing

corporations. Corporations must succeed in complex and unusually competitive global markets – competing not only in selling goods and services, but also in attracting capital and human resources.

◊ In the production of goods and services, corporations serve as an efficient instrument of co-operation among all the required resource providers, such as suppliers of capital, labour, intellectual property and various professional skills.

◊ By hosting relatively durable relations, corporations also form social networks. Long-term co-operation and resulting mutual dependencies among owners, managers, employees, suppliers, consumers, local communities, etc., create loyalties, expectations and understandings that go beyond pure market interaction.

◊ Corporations also serve wider national objectives. They mobilise the economic resources of a country across different regions and segments of society; they generate employment, income and training for citizens; they secure domestic supplies of goods, technologies and services; they provide tax income, foreign currency, etc.

42. The primary roles of the board of directors are to agree on a strategy for achieving the corporate objective and to hold management accountable for achieving that objective.

---

**THE CORPORATE OBJECTIVE AND THE ROLE OF THE BOARD**

*The corporate objective, and the role of the board of directors in achieving that objective, have been perceived distinctly in different societies. However, perceptions about the corporate objective and the role of board seem to be converging:*

• The objective of the corporation (and therefore of its management and board of directors) is to conduct its business activities so as to enhance corporate profit and shareholder gain. In pursuing this corporate objective, the board's role is to assume accountability for the success of the enterprise by taking responsibility for the management, in both failure and success. This means selecting a successful corporate management team, overseeing corporate strategy and performance, and acting as a resource for management in matters of planning and policy.

*Report of the National Association of Corporate Directors Commission on Director Professionalism, p. 1. (November 1996) (NACD Report on Director Professionalism).*

*.../..*

- The single overriding objective shared by all listed companies, whatever their size or type of business, is the preservation and the greatest practicable enhancement over time of their shareholders' investment. All boards have this responsibility and their policies, structure, composition and governing processes should reflect this.

*Final Report of the Hampel Committee on Corporate Governance*, at 1.16 (January 1998).

- The interest of the company may be understood as the overriding claim of the company considered as a separate economic agent, pursuing its own objectives which are distinct from those of shareholders, employees, creditors including the internal revenue authorities, suppliers and customers. It nonetheless represents the common interest of all these persons, which is for the company to remain in business and prosper. The Committee thus believes that directors should at all times be concerned solely to promote the interests of the company.

Conseil National du Patronat Français (CNPF) and Association Française des Entreprises Privées (AFEP*), The Boards of Directors of Listed Companies in France*, p. 5 (10 July 1995) *(Viénot Report).*

- In order to maintain and strengthen their international competitiveness into the twenty-first century in the context of an age of megacompetition, Japanese businesses must realise a form of corporate governance that meets global standards. Corporations are working on a regular basis to improve their management efficiency and to implement policies giving greater priority to stockholders' interests...

Keidanren (Japan Federation of Economic Organizations), *Urgent Recommendations Concerning Corporate Governance (Provisional)*, p. 1 (16 September 1997).

## 2.2 The Role of Formal Rules and Social Norms

43. In market economies, the corporation functions within a setting of formal rules and regulations as well as social norms and cultural traditions. Formal rules and regulations include contract, corporate, securities, antitrust, tax and intellectual property law, which all shape the economic interactions and functioning of the corporation. In addition, laws concerning health and safety, employment and environmental protection, to name but a few, clarify the social responsibilities of corporations. Social norms and cultural traditions also influence corporate missions and related governance practices.

44. The individual company must develop its own *modus operandi* to achieve economic profit and enhanced shareholder value within the boundary of this framework. Company-specific principles may be written into corporate

charters, articles of association, codes of behaviour, etc., or may simply be embedded in a strong corporate culture. In many cases, company-specific standards are shaped by time-tested values and the management principles of founding entrepreneurs and owners, as refined in interactions with networks of investors, employees, customers and local communities.

> *"The natural task for a corporation is to combine human and other resources to obtain the optimal result."*
>
> Mr. Keikichi Honda, Chairman and Representative Director, Nihon Sun Microsystems K.K. (Japan)
>
> *"The board's primary responsibility and objective should be to set an environment in which [the corporation's] business can prosper and grow for the long-term benefit of its shareholders."*
>
> Sir Ronald Hampel, Chairman ICI and Chairman of the Committee on Corporate Governance (United Kingdom)
>
> *"It is hard for me to imagine that a company can deliver superior shareholder returns over the long term without very positive relationships with other stakeholders, particularly its employees and suppliers."*
>
> Ms. Heidi Kunz, Chief Financial Officer, ITT Industries (United States)

45.     The interplay of formal rules and regulations, social norms and cultural traditions, and voluntary corporate practices results in a variety of corporate governance arrangements within and among OECD countries. Some of these practices have been demonstrated to be more competitive than others under given economic circumstances, and as a consequence are widely scrutinised and imitated.

## 2.3     General Principles Concerning the Corporate Mission

46.     The Advisory Group sets forth the following general principles regarding the mission of corporations, which support the other conclusions and recommendations in this Report:

◊   Generating economic profit so as to enhance shareholder value in the long term, by competing effectively, is the primary objective of corporations in market economies. Corporate governance must acknowledge this objective while simultaneously fulfilling broader economic, social and other national objectives. This multiplicity of functions is complex but necessary to the perpetuation of the corporation and the market system.

◊ Corporate governance must be responsive to global product, human resource and capital market competition. Governance practices that do not enable the corporation to meet the requirements and seize the opportunities of global competition cannot generate value for shareholders, and therefore cannot support other collective objectives.

◊ Different societies, cultures, enterprises and investors may have preferences for, and therefore pursue, projects and policies that promise a lesser economic return. When that is the case, such objectives should be effectively disclosed to investors, to markets and to other interested parties.

◊ Regulation is a legitimate device for aligning private incentives and collective objectives. However, regulation (including corporate law and investment regulation) is a powerful tool that should be used prudently and parsimoniously, as informed by regular testing of the relevance and economic impact of regulatory objectives.

◊ The board of directors has a critical role to play in ensuring that the corporation is managed so as to achieve its primary economic objective.

• • •

47.    The Advisory Group believes that further inquiry concerning the voluntary use and impact of disclosure as to the extent to which individual corporate objectives diverge from the primary economic objective may be useful.

# CORPORATE DISCLOSURE OF SOCIAL MISSION AND ITS POTENTIAL IMPACT

*The following are examples of how two publicly traded companies disclose social objectives that may have an impact on shareholder value.*

## Ben & Jerry's Homemade, Inc.

*Ben & Jerry's Homemade, Inc. is a publicly traded US company that expresses a commitment to a broad social mission, and for the last three years has devoted 7.5% of pre-tax profits to philanthropic purposes. The Company discloses the potential impact of its social mission to its shareholders in its Annual Report:*

- The Company's basic business philosophy is embodied in a three-part "mission statement", which includes a "social mission" to "operate the Company ... [to] improve the quality of life of our employees and a broad community: local, national and international". The Company believes that implementation of its social mission, which is integrated into the Company's business, has been beneficial to the Company's overall financial performance. However, it is possible that at some future date the amount of the Company's energies and resources devoted to its social mission could have a material adverse financial effect on the Company's business.

*Ben & Jerry's Homemade, Inc. Annual Report, p. 35 (1997).*

## The Body Shop

*The Body Shop, a publicly traded UK company, issues a "Stakeholder Report" concerning its social mission. The Report is based in part on a "social audit" and includes a description of "Next Steps" the Company intends to take in improving relations with employees, franchisees, suppliers, communities in which it operates and shareholders.*

Our reason for being:
- Dedicate our business to the pursuit of social and environmental change.
- Creatively balance the financial and human needs of our stakeholders: employees, customers, franchisees, suppliers and shareholders.
- Courageously ensure that our business is ecologically sustainable: meeting the needs of the present without compromising the future.
- Meaningfully contribute to local, national and international communities in which we trade, by adopting a code of conduct which ensures care, honesty, fairness and respect.
- Passionately campaign for the protection of the environment, human and civil rights, and against animal testing within the cosmetics and toiletries industry.
- Tirelessly work to narrow the gap between principle and practice, whilst making fun, passion and care part of our daily lives.

. . .

- We attempt to speak openly to shareholders about our business and to demonstrate that The Body Shop bottom line is not purely financial. This Stakeholder Report is a further step in this direction by attempting to present an integrated bottom line.

*The Body Shop Stakeholder Report, pp. 1, 26 (1997).*

# CHAPTER 3. ENSURING ADAPTABILITY OF CORPORATE GOVERNANCE ARRANGEMENTS

*The primary role for regulation is to shape a corporate governance environment, compatible with societal values, that allows competition and market forces to work so that corporations can succeed in generating long-term economic gain. Specific governance structures or practices will not necessarily fit all companies at all times. Nor should it be taken for granted that a given design may suit the same company during different stages of its development. For dynamic enterprises operating in a rapidly changing world, corporate governance adaptability and flexibility – supported by an enabling regulatory framework – is a prerequisite for better corporate performance.*

48.      Corporations need flexibility to respond successfully to rapid technological change and global competition in the markets for products, services and capital. In this context, a company's corporate governance arrangements must be adaptable to its specific business circumstances and the changing environment. In other words, no one corporate governance structure will fit all companies at all times.

49.      Corporations differ not only as to the skills and technology they need in order to remain competitive; they also have different needs as to the governance design that will best assist them in making the most efficient use of resources. As corporate needs change, the corporate governance arrangements of companies should be able to respond. In the absence of such adaptability, entrenched governance practices may limit the range of business relations and opportunities that an economy can successfully host.

50.      No single ownership or contracting structure will best serve the various forms of business enterprises in diverse business circumstances. Adaptability of corporate governance arrangements therefore appears to be an increasingly important prerequisite for economic dynamism.

51.     Because regulation is a powerful and potentially rigid tool, it should be used with care in the context of corporate governance, and reserved primarily for protecting the integrity and efficiency of capital markets.

> *"Governments have an important role in providing a solid framework for minimum corporate governance standards but should at the same time allow for more sophisticated investors and progressive corporations to apply higher standards on a voluntary basis."*
>
> Mr. Toshihiro Kiribuchi, Senior Corporate Advisor to the Board of Directors, OMRON Corporation (Japan)
>
> *"There should no doubt be a clear regulatory framework for business life. But as for the everyday work and governance by the board, I don't believe it should be articulated in the form of mandatory rules."*
>
> Mr. Michel Pebereau, Chairman and Chief Executive Officer, Banque Nationale de Paris (France)

52.     The Advisory Group views the following three conditions as essential to governance flexibility and adaptability:

◊   Permissive regulation, which allows for a range of ownership and contracting structures at the company level;

◊   Availability of alternative options for corporate governance arrangements; and

◊   Positive public attitudes toward diversity and innovation in the area of corporate governance.

## 3.1     Permissive Regulation

53.     Entrepreneurs, investors and corporations need the flexibility to craft governance arrangements that are responsive to unique business contexts so that corporations can respond to incessant change in technologies, competition, optimal firm organisation and vertical networking patterns. A market for governance arrangements should be permitted so that those arrangements that can attract investors and other resource contributors – and support competitive corporations – flourish.

54.     To obtain governance diversity, economic regulations, stock exchange rules and corporate law should support a range of ownership and governance forms. Over time, availability of "off-the-shelf" solutions will offer

benefits of market familiarity and learning, judicial enforceability and predictability.

---

**EVOLVING ORGANISATIONAL FORMS**

*Organisational forms for business entities continue to evolve. Recent examples include the following:*

- In 1994, France introduced a new form of limited liability incorporation – "Société par Actions Simplifiée" (S.A.S.) – having a less regulated governance structure than the classical "Société Anonyme" (S.A.). Compared to the S.A., founders of an S.A.S. have greater flexibility in determining: the structure and composition of the board; how board meetings will be held (including via telecommunications); rules for the general shareholders' meeting; terms of agreements between shareholders; terms of contracts with corporate officials; and means of disclosing information to shareholders. The new organisational form is reserved for closely held companies, founded by two or more business entities (not physical persons) with more than FF 1 500 000 paid in capital each. The availability of the S.A.S. form may encourage technological, industrial and other business joint ventures.

*Sources:* Various works, including D. Vidal, *Observations Sommaires sur la Loi du 4 Janvier 1994 Instituant la Société par Actions Simplifée, Les Petites Affiches,* 26 Janvier 1994 - No. 11.

- In 1997, the German Federal Supreme Court held that a corporation (GmbH) could serve as a general partner in a Kommanditgesellschaft auf Aktien (KGaA) – which combines elements of a stock corporation and a traditional partnership in a limited liability partnership with capital stock where only the general partner(s) are personally liable for the debts of the partnership. This has increased the attractiveness of the KGaA as a vehicle for maintaining control in family-owned businesses while meeting the entity's capital needs through the issuance of shares in the capital market. The KGaA has a supervisory board, but this organ lacks the authority to select the management board since management automatically lies with the general partners who have the authority to represent the company. As a general principle, the standard rules concerning shareholder rights apply to the KGaA, but these may be modified in certain instances by the Articles of Association.

*Source:* Dr. Dieter Feddersen, Feddersen Laule Scherzberg & Ohle Hansen Ewerwahn.

55.    Information about alternative ownership structures, financing vehicles, governance and board structures and processes, and contracting and remuneration schemes should be widely disseminated. At the company level, access to international experience and practice provides an important source of learning concerning improvements in corporate governance. Information about a wide range of governance practices is an important resource from which corporations can draw when modifying their own governance practices. Access to such information is also important for policy makers and regulators in their efforts to provide a suitable regulatory framework.

## 3.2    Availability of Alternative Options

56.    The need for flexibility and diversity in governance arrangements has many dimensions, including:

◊ *Ownership structure*: Ownership structure is a primary element in determining governance arrangements. Different ownership structures range from concentrated ownership by active owners to more dispersed ownership through domestic and international markets. Corporations can be owned by private entrepreneurs, controlled by founding families, closely held by a group of active partners, directed by holding companies, or subject to varying degrees of public ownership (ranging from large and influential owners to dispersed investors). Different forms of ownership are adapted to various business activities and competitive circumstances.

◊ *Legal organisational status*: Different structures include sole ownership, private company, limited liability partnership, closely held company, listed public company and holding company status.

◊ *Internal board structure:* Across companies, the role of the board (and its size and composition) varies according to ownership structure. For example, boards of publicly held corporations having multiple diffuse shareholders may be required to rely on outside and independent directors to monitor management; in a closely held corporation, a board comprised of investors may provide the necessary oversight.

◊ *Corporate ownership transactions*: Relevant transactions include mergers, acquisitions, divestitures, spin-offs, initial public offerings, management buy-outs, consolidation in holding companies, etc. (These restructurings may also implicate changes in organisational and ownership structures.)

◊   *Contracts with resource providers:* According to company-specific circumstances, there are differences in contracts with, and the remuneration of, various resource providers to the corporation.

57.    Changes in the corporate governance practices of individual corporations may alter the rights, interests and contracting terms of various resource providers. Therefore, it is important that such adjustments be effected with full disclosure, and in compliance with the existing formal, recognised rights of all parties.

58.    Corporate boards have a special responsibility in ensuring transparency, and protecting shareholder rights with respect to all corporate governance adjustments.

## 3.3    Public Acceptability of Governance Adjustments

59.    In some OECD countries, the ingrained local culture may favour uniformity over diversity and stability over change in governance arrangements.

60.    However, for an economy to maintain a competitive business sector, it is necessary to foster a positive perception of flexibility in corporate governance arrangements by highlighting the pivotal role flexibility plays in supporting entrepreneurship, growth and competitiveness across all sectors of society.

> *"The recent popular discovery of the principles of shareholder value in Germany proves that the cost of capital has become an important issue in corporate asset allocation and decision making."*
>
> Dr. Rolf-E. Breuer, Spokesman of the Board, Deutsche Bank AG (Germany)

●  ●  ●

61.    The Advisory Group believes that further inquiry concerning the use of alternative ownership structures, legal organisational forms and financing vehicles in OECD countries may be useful, particularly an international comparison of regulations, self-regulatory devices and desirable board practices associated with different types of organisational and ownership structures.

## PRIVATELY HELD *vs.* PUBLICLY TRADED BUSINESS ENTITIES

| Business entity type | Ownership, control and management | Benefits |
|---|---|---|
| Founding entrepreneurs, sole proprietorships, simple partnerships, wholly owned family businesses | The providers of ownership capital directly control and manage the enterprise. | Owners control the business directly. |
| Closely held (private) corporations | The providers of ownership capital control the enterprise either themselves or through a board of directors that they have direct representation on. They may also be involved in managing the business themselves, or may rely on professional managers. | Limited liability: aside from the equity investment, shareholder assets are not subject to the claims of corporate creditors; share-holders generally are protected from tort liability arising from corporate actions. |
| Nascent public-stock corporation | The providers of ownership capital of the private entity may still hold controlling interests in the firm that has just "gone public" by listing its stock. Some of these original capital providers may be members of the board and/or members of management. However, due to the presence of minority public shareholders, the board of directors gains importance in the control of the enterprise. | Continuity of firm existence: unlike partnerships and sole proprietorships, the corporation continues to exist despite the withdrawal of, or transfer of shares by, officers, directors, shareholders or employees. |
| Mature public-stock corporation | The diffuse, dispersed providers of ownership capital delegate control over the enterprise to a board of directors, and the board hires, compensates and, when necessary, replaces professional managers who run the business. | Free transferability of ownership interests and increased access to capital: capital can be raised through the issuance of stock; equity ownership interests can change hands – for public-stock companies, frequently in highly liquid markets – without necessarily changing corporate control and management. |

*A number of hybrid organisational forms have developed in various countries to capture various benefits associated with the traditional types of business entities listed above.*

*Source:* Weil, Gotshal & Manges LLP.

# CHAPTER 4. PROTECTING SHAREHOLDER RIGHTS

*For companies to attract equity investment, regulatory safeguards must emphasize fairness, transparency and accountability. These safeguards should take into account the new and growing category of non-controlling shareholders who have emerged in the form of institutional investors. The focus of current efforts to improve shareholder protection should centre on investor access to performance-related information, shareholder exercise of voting rights, and promotion of active and independent (non-executive) members of boards of directors to strengthen the quality of corporate governance.*

62.    Separation of corporate ownership from managerial control is the hallmark of the modern publicly traded corporation and raises long-recognised risks of divergent shareholder and management interests. OECD economies have produced a wide range of private contractual practices and statutory rules designed to protect shareholders by limiting these "agency costs". Such protections promote investor confidence and thereby help increase the flow of private investment capital to the business sector.

63.    Insufficient shareholder protection may lead to decreased access to capital, increased capital costs and lower investment levels in the economy. Therefore, companies, investors and policy makers have a collective interest in promoting adequate protections for domestic and foreign shareholders. Improvements in shareholder protection have direct benefits for companies seeking to attract investors and decrease their capital costs. Since improvements in shareholder protection are in the company's own interest, competition for funds can be expected to have an immediate impact on the diffusion of these safeguards.

64.    Two specific types of "agency costs" need to be minimised to protect shareholders adequately: *i)* management discretion needs to be limited as to the risk of non-profitable use of equity funds, and *ii)* transfers of assets from minority to controlling shareholders need to be subject to strict fairness

requirements. Most OECD countries have developed statutory rules and private contractual practices to address these problems.

65.     Effective shareholder protection stresses: *i) fairness*, through regulations prohibiting fraud, managerial or controlling shareholder self-dealing, and other "insider" wrongdoing; *ii) accountability*, through clearly set-forth governance roles and responsibilities and primary reliance on managerial monitoring by a board of directors; and *iii) transparency*, through regulations that mandate the disclosure of information to shareholders.

66.     Although class action and derivative litigation provides a means of enforcing shareholder rights, its availability should be balanced against the cost of artificial constraints on the entrepreneurial incentives of managers, directors and owners. Many countries have refined regulations in this area, with provisions to protect against litigation abuse in the form of tests for the sufficiency of shareholder complaints, and safe harbours for management and director actions (such as the business judgement rule), as well as safe harbours for the disclosure of information.

67.     Disclosure is an especially important and efficient means of protecting shareholders and is at the heart of corporate governance. Adequate and timely information about corporate performance enables investors to make informed buy-and-sell decisions and thereby helps the market reflect the value of a corporation under present management. If the market determines that current management is not performing, a decrease in stock price will sanction management's failure and open the way to management changes. Adequate and timely information also enables investors to make considered judgements about the quality of management and – short of buy-sell decisions – whether or not to use their ownership influence to seek a change in management behaviour. Both exit of investment from underperforming companies and investor pressure are important mechanisms for maintaining corporate governance discipline in publicly traded corporations. Given the obvious interest of shareholders in assuring themselves of excellent management, management itself should value shareholders' appraisals of management quality – to avoid "investor exit" and its negative effect on the company's market valuation, as well as to avoid negative relations with existing investors.

68.     In the past decade, institutional investors (pension funds, life insurance companies, mutual funds, etc.) have emerged as the dominant suppliers of equity capital. These institutions – with diversified portfolios including small but significant stakes in a large number of companies – cannot

rely fully on the classic safeguard of selling underperforming securities because of the size of their holdings and their portfolio indexing strategies.

69.     In the new economic environment, the most effective focus of efforts to improve the protection of both individual and institutional shareholders' rights centres on: access to performance-related information, shareholder participation (and vote) in annual general meetings, and an active, independent board of directors.

## 4.1     Improving the Disclosure of Information

70.     Requirements concerning the disclosure of relevant corporate financial information have taken shape over decades, and currently provide a basically sound framework in most OECD countries.

71.     In response to increased complexity in the valuation of corporate assets, ongoing improvements in information disclosure techniques and formats promise to decrease the cost and improve the quality of information available to investors. Regulatory frameworks should enable and encourage progress in this area.

72.     Notably, new information technologies offer the potential for improvements in the accessibility, frequency and content of information shared with investors. In particular, information technologies may improve individual shareholders' access to timely, relevant information. Increased availability of corporate information improves the ability of investors and analysts to evaluate corporate performance.

73.     Significant initiatives to improve the quality, reliability and comparability of financial information disclosed by corporations are under way in individual OECD countries and at the international level. Initiatives in the area of accounting standards seek to increase investor confidence and reduce costs in processing disclosed information for transnational investments. Global efforts to conform accounting standards should be useful in improving international comparability of accounts. *[The Advisory Group notes concurrent work within the International Accounting Standards Committee (IASC), and by the US Financial Accounting Standards Board (FASB), which determines US Generally Accepted Accounting Principles (US-GAAP).]*

74.     In addition to financial information about past performance, investors increasingly value information concerning the corporation's future prospects, opportunities and risks as well as non-financial information about "intangible assets" that may be important to the competitive performance of corporations. Such "intangible assets" may include governance arrangements, management structures, compensation and pay procedures, human capital practices such as training and employee relations, intellectual property ownership and protection methods, quality of products, brand image, and consumer satisfaction and goodwill. Recognising the value investors may place on such qualitative indicators of corporate performance, corporations are beginning to innovate by disclosing such information to investors, but the formats, techniques and quantitative indicators of such disclosures remain experimental.

75.     Traditional concerns for protecting shareholders from inaccurate, unreliable or fraudulent information need to be balanced with the potential value to be had from forward-looking and non-financial information, which by definition are types of information that are less certain and verifiable than historic accounting information. However, disclosure of forward-looking or non-financial information about intangible assets may raise problems of legal liability when predictions are not met or verification is difficult. Clearly defined disclosure safe harbours in regulatory systems may promote less risky and more efficient diffusion and use of forward-looking and non-financial information.

76.     In some OECD economies, regulations or stock exchange listing rules have been enacted, or are being considered, to require systematic disclosure of information on corporate governance procedures and other intangible assets. However, voluntary corporate innovations in the exchange of such information within the private sector – at both national and international levels – are likely to be the main engine for improvements. Disclosure formats in this area are evolving too rapidly to be mandated by regulations.

77.    A major source of corporate information is provided by various stock analysts and rating services that continuously screen, analyse and disseminate relevant information to investors. Stock analysis and rating services gain importance as information needs become more complex, and depend on rapidly changing market conditions. Innovation and competition in these services add to the availability of relevant information.

78.    International competition among stock analysts and rating services is likely to increase the quality, integrity and fully competitive supply of stock analysis and rating services. Companies can increase the quality and decrease the cost of investor monitoring by co-operating with analysts.

---

**INTERNATIONAL DISCLOSURE TRENDS**

- Outside the United States, corporations are feeling pressure to bring disclosure up to US standards. This is motivated by regulators or stock exchanges seeking to increase transparency to attract foreign capital. In addition, market forces are compelling many companies in Europe and elsewhere to seek capital from global equity investors, who demand greater disclosure. This is causing more openness in the traditionally close relationships between companies and institutional investors, especially banks, in European countries such as the United Kingdom and Germany.

- These traditionally close relationships outside the United States (which have involved considerable exchange of strategic performance information) may be somewhat modified or curtailed under new disclosure laws in various countries. At the same time, more in-depth communications are being encouraged in the United States, under pressures from activist institutional investors or through initiatives like the safe harbour legislation.

- The result will probably be a move toward the centre, with US companies more involved in strategic discussions with their major investors, and non-US companies more transparent about their discussions with their major investors.

The Conference Board, *Communicating Corporate Performance: A Delicate Balance,* Special Research Report No. 97-1, p. 45 (1997).

---

## 4.2    Encouraging Shareholder Participation

79.    The Advisory Group recognises the right to vote and participate in annual meetings that is generally associated with share ownership as an important investor asset. However, many shareholders do not make use of their voting rights. This may be explained in part by the fact that the costs of monitoring corporate performance accrue only to the shareholders who are engaged in the monitoring, while the benefits are shared by the entire

shareholder base. The large size of institutional holdings may justify a more assertive use of these rights (as the break-even point of fixed-cost/variable-benefit trade-offs will shift). However, many institutions and fund managers still have strong incentives to avoid the costs related to more active participation.

> *"As institutional investors with more than one thousand different shares in our portfolio, we cannot be involved in all the companies we own. Therefore, our role as institutional investor should be to influence corporate governance over the market."*
>
> Kimitoshi Hasegawa, Managing Director, Dai-ichi Life Research Institute Inc. (Japan)

80.     To encourage institutional shareholders to vote, some regulators have emphasized that the use of voting rights is part of the fiduciary responsibilities of intermediary agents. Some countries have made proxy delegations between individuals and institutions in certain circumstances subject to explicit approval by principals, while other countries contemplate facilitating custodians' voting. The discussion of appropriate regulatory efforts to encourage institutional shareholders to vote has also included proposals to make such voting compulsory, as well as to encourage such voting through tax incentives. The economics and politics of such reform proposals are complex, but sound common principles should be identified.

81.     Institutional investors compete with one another domestically and internationally, in the management of savings plans and retirement and pension funds. Transparency of institutional voting policies is important to accountability in the exercise of investor rights.

82.     Diverse initiatives are underway in many OECD countries to streamline voting procedures. National regulations nevertheless differ as to time delays and deadlines in proxy delegations, and the costs these may impose on non-controlling shareholders who want to participate in governance.

83.     Distribution of financial reports and shareholders' meeting documentation has always been a costly and time-consuming task. Information technologies provide new possibilities in this regard. The organisation of shareholders' meetings and voting procedures may also benefit from information technologies. Technical and regulatory adjustments may be necessary for such innovations.

## THE RIGHT TO VOTE: A VALUABLE ASSET

*There is growing recognition that the right to vote associated with stock ownership is a valuable asset:*

- Institutional shareholders have a responsibility to make considered use of their votes.

*Final Report of the Hampel Committee on Corporate Governance*, at 2.14 (January 1998).

- The French Commission des Opérations de Bourse and the French association of fund managers have recommended in their rules of conduct that fund managers exercise their voting rights and report on their record of actively voting their proxies in the annual report of the fund they manage.

*Sources:* Commission des Opérations de Bourse; AFG-ASFFI, *règlement de déontologie des OPCVM,* article 15, p. 9 (3 April 1997).

- In July 1994, the US Department of Labor issued Interpretive Bulletin 94-2 emphasizing that the voting of proxies is a fiduciary responsibility of plan asset management. "Plan fiduciaries have a responsibility to vote proxies on issues that may affect the value of the shares in the plan's portfolio... [T]he responsible fiduciary [is required] to weigh the costs and benefits of voting on proxy proposals relating to foreign securities and make an informed decision with respect to whether voting a given proxy proposal is prudent and solely in the interest of the plan's participants and beneficiaries."

*Source:* US Department of Labor, Pension and Welfare Benefits Administration, *Interpretive Bulletin 94-2, 29 CFR Part 2509* (29 July 1994)

*Although not directly subject to the US Department of Labor's Interpretive Bulletin 94-2, the California Public Employee Retirement System (CalPERS) – the largest US public pension fund with US$126 billion in assets – recognises that the right to vote is a valuable asset and has begun to actively vote its international equity proxies:*

- For fiscal 1996-97, CalPERS voted on proxies of approximately 780 international companies with an aggregate market value of US$23.7 billion. Among international firms [CalPERS] voted against management proposals... in Switzerland, Thailand, Brazil and Malaysia, once each; Australia, Germany, Spain and Singapore, twice each; Hong Kong and South Africa, three times each; Japan and the United Kingdom, six each; Philippines, seven; the Netherlands, nine; Korea, 10; Indonesia, 15 times; and France, 33 times. Most of its negative votes on international proxies involved increases in equity capital issued without pre-emptive rights to existing shareholders, use of all the authorised capital to ward off hostile take-overs and amending articles of incorporation where no pertinent information was provided.

*Source: Pensions & Investments* (27 October 1997).

## 4.3 Promoting Active and Independent Board Members

84.     In publicly traded corporations, the board of directors is elected by shareholders to monitor management at a closer level than dispersed shareholders can achieve. By monitoring management, the board guards against fraud, waste of assets, underperformance and, more generally, the agency problem.

85.     The increased importance of the board's role is highlighted in modern corporations because of the strategic intricacies of management matters, the need for confidentiality (especially in high-technology and high-competition markets), the difficulty of evaluating management achievements and performance in adverse economic circumstances and the sizeable commercial risks inherent in increasing numbers of company activities and investments.

86.     The presence of active and independent members of the board of directors – creating a "professional" board in the sense of a board composed of dedicated, informed, active and independent individuals (but not in the sense of full-time directors devoted solely to monitoring management) – is an economic solution that addresses simultaneously the agency problem and the technical complexities, confidentiality concerns and rapid response requirements inherent in monitoring managerial performance.

87.     The active, independent board is an evolving concept and design that has emerged in many OECD economies over the past decade. While the structure of corporate boards differs among OECD nations, and includes both single-tier and two-tier boards, improvements in independence can be implemented in any type of board system. Of course, cultural adjustments may be necessary and may result in the development of different types of independence mechanisms. For example, in Japan greater reliance on the role of a board of auditors having non-executive and independent members may develop along the lines recommended by Keidanren (Japan Federation of Economic Organizations).

88.     Strategies for improving board independence have been introduced by a number of companies; various professional groups and committees across countries have articulated board "best practices" to provide guidance for corporate initiatives; and certain stock exchanges have imposed listing requirements concerning board composition, structure and practice and have mandated disclosure of governance practices. However, the task of establishing efficient, active and independent boards as a strategy for attracting investors

and lowering the cost of equity capital is largely one for individual companies to undertake.

---

### ROLE SIMILARITY IN SINGLE- AND TWO-TIER BOARD SYSTEMS

#### *Shareholders Annual General Meeting*

Determines fundamental issues, such as:

- Selecting the outside auditing firm; and
- Selecting the board of directors (single-tier) or the supervisory board of directors (two-tier)

| *Single-tier* *Board of Directors* | *Two-tier* *Supervisory Board* |
|---|---|

- Selects, evaluates and compensates members of senior management (single-tier) or executive board (two-tier)
- Guides corporate strategy
- Oversees corporate performance
- Approves certain important decisions of senior management or executive board body

| *Senior Management* | *Executive Board* |
|---|---|

Under the direction of the board of directors (single-tier) or supervisory board (two-tier):

- Executes corporate strategy
- Manages the operations of the company

*Source:* Weil, Gotshal & Manges LLP.

---

89.     The Advisory Group recognises that the structure and specific mandate of the board varies across countries. Despite such differences, the Advisory Group believes that a set of common principles can improve the quality of board function, regardless of particular circumstances. The Advisory Group notes that these principles may also apply to organisations in the not-for-profit sector.

90.     As a starting point, the Advisory Group notes that members of the board of directors are generally recognised to be fiduciaries to the corporation and its shareholders. The individual and collective legal liabilities of directors need to be balanced with protections for entrepreneurial action under sufficient "business judgement" safe harbours.

91.     Drawing on recent and ongoing efforts in OECD countries, the Advisory Group has identified what it considers as the most important features of an active, independent "professional" board.

◊ *Leadership in corporate strategy:* The board should guide and participate in the basic strategic choices of the corporation. The board should understand the inherent prospects and risks of the strategic choices of the corporation, and in co-operation with management, should develop a set of benchmarks for monitoring the success of the strategic plan. This requires that board members have a high level of professional experience and a background that is suitable to the corporate objective. To provide the necessary integrity and stability in the long-term direction of company affairs, the board should develop a collective understanding on matters of critical importance to the quality and credibility of its decisions. However, such constructive collegiality should not inhibit openness in discussions, diversity of views and independent assessment by individual directors during the decision-making process.

◊ *Active oversight of management:* The board's primary task is to monitor management and hold it accountable in achieving the corporation's primary objective. This requires that the board actively engage in supervising, motivating and evaluating management. Under certain circumstances, this will require replacing non-performing management. As part of this task, the board should aim at reinforcing perceptions of trust and fairness between management and board members as well as establishing a succession plan for top management.

◊ *Independence:* To oversee management, a board must develop and voice an objective judgement on corporate affairs, independently from management. It is conceptually difficult for members of management to be independent of management, especially as to active oversight of management. Specific board structures and practices may assist in promoting independence, such as having a quantitative majority of directors who are not affiliated with management (outside directors), appointing a non-executive director as board chairman or, in the alternative, designating an independent board "leader". Certain tasks suited to independent judgements may be delegated to specialised board committees comprised exclusively of outside directors. Such wholly independent committees are becoming widespread for addressing audit, executive compensation and director nomination functions. Certain stock exchanges may require certain types of committees and committee composition – mainly in the area of auditing – as part of their listing requirements. In general, creating sufficient board independence and independent board leadership and relying on independent board committees are matters that may depend on each company's needs, as well as existing national practices, and investor pressure may cause modifications of both individual corporate and national practices.

◊ *Oversight of the audit function:* The board bears the ultimate responsibility for the integrity of the corporation's financial disclosure – which requires reviewing and approving the annual report, and the periodical financial accounts of the corporation – as well as the responsibility for the corporation's general compliance with law. This is a cornerstone of good corporate governance and the main instrument of accountability of boards to shareholders. In ensuring that the corporation's accounts are kept and communicated in an objective, reliable and informative fashion, the board should co-operate with external professional auditors to improve the reporting system and interpret accurately the performance indicators of the corporation. The board audit function may also include the design and evaluation of complementary non-financial indicators that contribute to an accurate picture of the corporation's tangible and intangible assets, competitive positions and prospects in markets. The board should make sure that the proper reporting structures and routines adapted to the circumstances of the corporation are in place.

◊ *Control of director nomination:* The selection of a slate of board member nominees – for presentation to the shareholders for vote at the annual meeting – is an important board task that implicates board independence and accountability to shareholders. While it may be appropriate for management to confer on the selection of an appropriate slate of board candidates, the ultimate selection should be determined by the board. In some OECD nations, this task is increasingly overseen by directors who are not members of management.

◊ *Accountability to shareholders and society:* The board should acknowledge, assess and further the internal and external "citizenship" responsibilities of the corporation. While being accountable to the shareholders, it should also be responsive to the concerns of other parties affected by corporate actions. The board should ensure ethical behaviour and compliance with laws and regulations in all areas and countries in which the company operates.

◊ *Regular self-evaluation:* Finally, the board should evaluate its own performance in a continuing effort to improve. For this purpose, the board should establish criteria for board and board member performance, and pursue a self-evaluation process for evaluating both overall board performance and the contributions of individual directors. Developing these procedures is a new challenge for many boards. Guidance is available from a number of individual companies and professional associations that have developed evaluation processes recently.

92.     These seven principles concerning the board's role and the need for board independence should serve as the basis for company-specific initiatives to improve board governance – a task that should be left to the initiatives of individual companies. National examples of efforts to assist this process are listed in Annex 2 and include among many others, the Viénot Report in France, the Dey Report in Canada, the Bosch Report in Australia, the Cadbury Code and Hampel Report in the United Kingdom, and the Report of the National Association of Corporate Directors Commission on Director Professionalism and The Business Roundtable Statement on Corporate Governance in the United States. Distilling basic principles from such reports has immense value in the educational process of building an active and independent board culture. However, as these reports recognise, mandating detailed board governance practices is unnecessary and may even be counterproductive.

---

*"Since statutory law doesn't, and shouldn't, give any detailed instructions about the work of the board, it is extremely important that the companies themselves explicitly formulate the standards so that every board member knows exactly what is expected of them as individuals and as a board as a whole."*

Mr. Jonathan Charkham, past member of the Cadbury Committee and previously Advisor to the Governor of the Bank of England (United Kingdom)

*"The strength of non-mandatory board best practices and guidelines lies in their voluntary and flexible nature."*

Mr. Gregory E. Lau, Executive Director of Worldwide Executive Compensation and Corporate Governance, General Motors Corporation (United States)

---

93.     The Advisory Group believes it useful to further distil and consolidate the concept of the independent "professional" board, and to develop a common understanding among investors, companies and stock exchange authorities (as well as professional associations and representatives of all of these parties).

Knowledge pertaining to board composition, organisation and process is valuable. Therefore, efforts to collect, discuss and disseminate information about board "best practices" – and to forge a common understanding among investors, companies and regulators at national and international levels – should be encouraged.

---

### NON-EXECUTIVE AND INDEPENDENT BOARD MEMBERS

*In the United States, although not required by law or listing requirements, it is generally agreed that it is "best practice" for boards of publicly traded corporations to include a majority of non-executive directors who are capable of exercising judgement independent of management. See NACD Report on Director Professionalism, at 9-10; and The Business Roundtable, Statement on Corporate Governance at 13-14 (September 1997). A general consensus is developing throughout a number of other countries that boards of publicly traded companies should include at least some non-executive members who are capable of exercising judgement independent of management:*

- [T]he boards of listed public companies should include a majority of non-executive directors... The majority of non-executive directors should preferably be independent, not only of management but of any other external influence that could detract from their ability to act in the interests of the company as a whole.

Working Group representing Australian Institute of Company Directors, Australian Society of Certified Practising Accountants, Business Council of Australia, Law Council of Australia, The Institute of Chartered Accountants in Australia and The Securities Institute of Australia, *Corporate Practices and Conduct*, Guideline 1.1 (3rd ed., 1995) (*Bosch Report*).

- The notion of independent director is not only opposed to that of executive director, it is also opposed to that of any director with any sort of special interest in the company, whether as a shareholder, a supplier or a customer. [T]he boards of all listed companies should have at least two independent members, although it is up to each board to determine the most appropriate balance in its membership.

Conseil National du Patronat Français (CNPF) and Association Française des Entreprises Privées (AFEP), *The Boards of Directors of Listed Companies in France*, pp. 11, 12 (10 July 1995) (*Viénot Report*).

- Any listed companies with a turnover of Rs.100 crores and above should have professionally competent and acclaimed non-executive directors, who should constitute: (1) at least 30 per cent of the board if the Chairman of the company is a non-executive director; or (2) at least 50 per cent of the board if the Chairman and Managing Director is the same person.

Confederation of Indian Industry, *Desirable Corporate Governance: A Code*, Recommendation 2 (April 1997).

- The board should include non-executive directors of sufficient calibre and number for their views to carry significant weight in the board's decision... The majority [of non-executive directors] should be independent of management and free from any business or other relationship which could materially interfere with the exercise of their independent judgement, apart from their fees and shareholding.

*Report of the Committee on the Financial Aspects of Corporate Governance, Code of Best Practice*, at 2.2 (1 December 1992) (*Cadbury Report*). See also *Final Report of the Hampel Committee on Corporate Governance*, at Principle III and 2.5 (January 1998).

# BOARD INDEPENDENCE AND AUDIT COMMITTEES

*Independent board audit committees – and, in Japan, the board of auditors – can provide a valuable means of ensuring accountability to shareholders.*

- The Corporation Law has already been revised to strengthen the authority of corporate auditors. However, ... their independence from the board of directors and the solidity of their status [need to be] secured. It is therefore necessary to carry out the following improvements, directed in principle at all companies listed on domestic stock exchanges or registered for trading on the over-the-counter market.

  (1)     Stricter requirements concerning outside auditors: Under the existing Corporation Law, at least, an auditor must have been a person other than a director, manager, or employee of the corporation in the five years immediately before assuming the post. This provision should be changed to exclude anyone who has ever been a director, manager, or employee of the corporation or a subsidiary thereof.

  (2)     Increase in number of outside auditors: The present requirement that there be at least one outside auditor should be strengthened to a requirement that when auditors are appointed, at least half must be outsiders at any annual meeting of shareholders.

Keidanren (Japan Federation of Economic Organizations), *Urgent Recommendations Concerning Corporate Governance (Provisional)*, paragraphs 1(1) and 1(2) (16 September 1997).

- Since 1978, the New York Stock Exchange ("NYSE") has required that all listed companies have a board of directors audit committee wholly comprised of independent directors. The NYSE generally defines "independent directors" as persons who are "independent of management and free from any relationship that, in the opinion of its board of directors, would interfere with the exercise of independent judgement as a committee member." The American Stock Exchange ("ASE") and the National Association of Securities Dealers Automated Quotation System ("NASDAQ") generally require listed companies to have audit committees comprised of at least a majority of independent directors.

New York Stock Exchange, *Listed Company Manual*, 3-1 (1991); American Stock Exchange, *Company Guide*, 1-12 (1992); National Association of Securities Dealers, *NASD Manual: Schedules to the By-Laws* (CCH) paragraph 1812, p. 1580 (1994).

- In 1992, the Cadbury Committee (UK) recommended that all companies listed on the London Stock Exchange establish a board audit committee of non-executive directors. It further recommended that the majority of non-executive directors serving on the committee should be independent. "[Independence] means that apart from their directors' fees and shareholdings, [directors] should be independent of management and free from any business or other relationship which could materially interfere with the exercise of their independent judgement." The recent Hampel Committee Report (UK) supports the Cadbury Report's recommendation.

*Report of the Committee on the Financial Aspects of Corporate Governance, Code of Best Practice*, at 4.35 and 4.12 (1 December 1992) (*Cadbury Report*); *Final Report of the Hampel Committee on Corporate Governance*, at 2.21 (January 1998).

● ● ●

94.　　The Advisory Group believes that further inquiry concerning comparisons of individual OECD country practices, and the impact of such practices may be useful, as relates to:

◊　regulatory efforts to protect shareholder rights through the use and enforcement of securities and market regulations while guarding against litigation abuse;

◊　contractual enforcement capabilities;

◊　the legal standards that govern shareholder, director and management authority and accountability (fiduciary duties and legal liabilities);

◊　the comparability, reliability, confidentiality, enforcement and safe-harbour issues related to accurate, timely disclosure – in the context of global capital markets – of both historic and forward-looking corporate financial information;

◊　the disclosure of information on corporate ownership structure, corporate governance procedures and relevant non-financial information concerning intangible assets;

◊　regulatory efforts to protect, enforce and promote shareholders' rights to vote at and participate in annual general meetings. In particular, study of the impact of regulation on the investment strategies of institutional investors and their use of voting rights would be useful; and

◊　corporate board independence in individual OECD countries, including stock exchange listing requirements and various regulatory and voluntary efforts to define "independence" and to emphasize the use of independent board members and auditors.

# CHAPTER 5. ENABLING ACTIVE INVESTING

*Active owners can play a distinct role in strengthening a corporation's ability to exploit new business opportunities. Such active investment should be encouraged, but with adequate protections for more passive holders.*

95.      The direct participation of equity investors in monitoring corporation performance can reduce agency costs, and may at times enable an enterprise to follow strategic and competitive objectives that less-involved investors might view as unduly risky. Active investors can provide managerial and entrepreneurial impetus to corporations while committing large amounts of additional capital for complex investment projects that would otherwise be difficult to sell to diffuse and passive investors. They also may be more amenable to a higher degree of risk and help to contain risk through active involvement with management.

96.      The prototypical active investment involves the entrepreneur who devotes his or her capital to researching and developing – and then bringing to market – a new product or commercial idea. Active equity investors are commonly associated with privately held, often family-controlled businesses, that are wholly or majority-owned by a large investor or investor group. (Generally, such privately held companies are subject to rules designed to protect minority shareholders, if they have such shareholders.) Other types of privately held active investment include investments in high-risk technology start-ups by venture capitalists, investments by specialised equity funds or partners in the funding of managerial spin-offs from large corporations, and other management buy-out funds. In publicly traded companies, active investors typically hold large – but not necessarily majority – positions.

97.      Active investment may be particularly well-suited to capitalising on opportunities that require continual monitoring due to their potential high risk, and to supporting businesses experiencing serious difficulty. Such businesses frequently require investor attention to undertake necessary in-depth restructuring of their strategy and internal organisation. Both of these opportunities are common in a high-technology, highly competitive economy.

98.     Notwithstanding its positive contributions to the monitoring and governance of corporations, active investing may implicate concerns about insider trading and unfair wealth transfers. Regulators can limit potential risks through well-balanced corporate law and securities rules enforcement.

> *"Controlling shareholders that can match internal management expertise provide an extremely efficient way to reduce agency costs and should not be discouraged ex ante. What is important is to support the sustainability of such active ownership arrangements by designing devices that properly protect the rights of minority owners."*
>
> Mr. Woong Soon Song, Senior Managing Director of Samsung Electronics Co., Ltd. (Korea)

99.     Active investors are often coupled with other tiers of financing extended by more passive investors. Dual classes of equity, or equity accompanied by convertible bonds, non-voting equity or limited liability partnerships are fairly common methods of coupling active investors with more passive, less risky investment instruments. However, instruments that have a status different from full-fledged equity may necessitate stronger contractual protections.

100.     Active investors and more passive investors may have a common interest in the use of such instruments. Active investors may benefit from additional funding, while passive investors can take advantage of the lower monitoring costs and, possibly, more stable returns of these complementary financings. Some investors may view the use of such instruments as a departure from "one share, one vote" principles, while others may accept their utility as financing instruments with distinct risk/return profiles.

> *"It is likely that the quality of corporate governance would improve if the regulatory framework more explicitly takes into account the distinct but complementary roles played by arm's length diversified investors and active investors with significant stakes in individual companies respectively."*
>
> Mr. Lennart Låftman, Managing Director, Swedish National Pension Fund, 5th Board (Sweden)
>
> *"If arm's length investors and active investors are both engaged in a company, I would prefer the use of two different investment vehicles for the different kinds of investors since their expectations, value-added and information needs are so different."*
>
> Dr. Bernhard Wunderlin, Managing Director, Harald Quandt Holding GmbH (Germany)

## 5.1    Regulation of Active Ownership

101.    The Advisory Group recognises that there are a variety of forms of active investing in modern economies, characterised by distinct financing vehicles, ownership structures, governance arrangements and contractual relations among different groups of investors. The Advisory Group believes the availability of these options should be preserved to allow flexibility in addressing the complex governance challenges of modern economies.

102.    Active investors may, or may not, seek direct board participation and legal "insider" status. Although active investor involvement in monitoring management can benefit all shareholders and mitigate traditional agency problems, certain basic legal protections for minority shareholders must be in place to guard against potential abuses, such as dilution, fraud and insider trading.

---

*"As a large institutional investor we don't believe in micromanagement of companies... We will demand certain standards, certain information and certain structures of companies and in return we will offer long-term support to companies."*

Mr. Alastair Ross Goobey, Chief Executive Officer, Hermes (United Kingdom)

*"For active investors as ourselves, standard company information is clearly necessary but only the starting point. Because of our long-term view, we often insist on having a level of understanding about the company that is not readily available to the public. This brings legal restrictions on our ability to sell our stock in troubled companies and in fact forces us to get actively involved rather than just pulling out."*

Ms. Nancy B. Peretsman, Executive Vice President and Managing Director, Allen & Company Inc. (United States)

---

103.    Large equity positions in publicly traded companies are already highly regulated in some OECD economies. Some countries prevent or discourage active participation by investors who hold less than 100 per cent of a company's stock. For example, some security regulations may require investors reaching certain ownership thresholds to bid for all the remaining shares of a company or to simply disclose ownership positions and intent.

104.    Active investing by venture capitalists or leveraged buy-out funds in private, non-listed companies tends to be less subject to regulation because of the absence of minority investors: active investors reap the costs and benefits of the strategic actions they advocate. Of course, such relations between investors

and enterprises tend to be more open-ended and less standardised, and therefore carry higher risks. In spite of these higher risks, private equity investment has increased in OECD economies.

105.     Active investing can involve the use of holding companies, through which an entity owns an interest in a range of distinct business lines and affiliates – each of which may issue its own equity securities. While in certain countries this form has been limited, because of concerns about excessive power, insufficient transparency and wealth-transfer risks from non-controlling investors, it has worked well in some OECD countries such as the United States. Certain other countries have liberalised their regulations in this area. For instance, Japan has recently begun to permit the use of holding companies. As with traditional "active investing," basic legal protections are needed to safeguard minority investors in the holding company and its subsidiaries.

---

**PROTECTING MINORITY SHAREHOLDERS UNDER GERMAN LAW**

The law on industrial groups (Konzernrecht) has a paramount importance in German corporate law. This law is stipulated in the German Stock Corporation Act that contains rules for industrial group relations and the associated provisions for the protection of minority shareholders.

The most important rules from this perspective are the "control agreement" and the "profit-and-loss transfer agreement". In a control agreement, the management of a stock corporation is imputed to another company. A profit-and-loss transfer agreement implies that all profits of a stock corporation are transferred to another company and that the controlling company is obliged to set off the annual losses of the controlled stock corporation.

The protection of minority shareholders is twofold. Firstly, the conclusion of a control agreement or a profit-and-loss transfer agreement requires the consent of the shareholders' meeting, adopted by a qualified majority and the minority shareholders have certain specified information rights. The profit-and-loss transfer agreement as well as the control agreement must provide for a guaranteed dividend which is to be paid to the minority shareholders. Secondly, the controlling company is obliged to make an offer to the minority shareholders of the subsidiary company to acquire their shares either for cash or in exchange for shares in the controlling company, on the basis of a fair evaluation of the controlled stock corporation.

*Source:* Dr. Dieter Feddersen, Feddersen Laule Scherzberg & Ohle Hansen Ewerwahn.

---

## FORMS OF ACTIVE INVESTING

A wide variety of active investing strategies and forms have arisen to provide closer supervision of investor assets. One example is the private equity partnership in which capital is pooled, frequently in the form of limited liability partnerships, where the general partners identify the investment opportunities and carry out the active work. The remaining capital is provided by other individual investors, or institutional investors who, as limited partners gain residual returns from the investments.

Although more common in the United States, in Europe, Doughty Hanson has arranged successful cross-border restructurings including a joint venture between French company Pechiney and German company Schmalbach-Lubeca.

*Sources:* C. Kester & T. Luehrman, "Rehabilitating the Leveraged Buyout", *Harvard Business Review* (May-June 1995); "Taking a Lever to Europe", *Euromoney* (October 1997).

In Sweden, Investor AB exemplifies another form of active ownership. Investor AB is a listed industrial holding company that holds substantial stakes in several public companies, including Ericsson and Astra. Its objective is to generate shareholder value through long-term active ownership, active investment operations and trading. Over the past 25 years, the average total annual return to Investor AB shareholders has exceeded 20 per cent.

*Source:* Investor AB.

Many institutional investors with more arm's length investment strategies have recognised the potential profitability of investment vehicles specialised in active investing. CalPERS recently announced a US$200 million limited partnership agreement with the British active fund Active Value Capital LP:

"This ... fit[s] with our philosophy that appropriate corporate governance practices have a positive effect on a company's performance. We believe Active Value has the ability to unlock shareholder value. They have a proven track record in bringing good returns on their investments." *California Public Employees' Retirement System, Press Release, 26 January 1998.*

● ● ●

106.    The Advisory Group believes that further inquiry concerning different forms of active investing in both public and private companies may be useful, in particular, concerning comparisons of individual OECD country experiences related to:

◊   the regulatory issues raised by active investing, including the extent to which securities, tax and other regulations can impede or enhance active investing; and

◊   how the different forms of active investing contribute to capital allocation and improved corporate governance, and the development, diffusion and regulation of complementary financing vehicles which accompany active investing.

# CHAPTER 6. ALIGNING THE INTERESTS OF SHAREHOLDERS AND OTHER STAKEHOLDERS

*Corporate success is linked to the ability to align the interests of directors, managers and employees with the interests of shareholders. Performance-based compensation is a useful tool for this purpose. Independent (non-executive) members of the board of directors – or in certain nations, board of auditors – have a special responsibility in designing and approving appropriate remuneration schemes.*

107.     To maximise individual and collective contributions and reduce the agency costs inherent in the modern corporation's ownership structure, effective corporate governance needs to align the interests of the core resource providers – shareholders, directors, managers and employees – whose efforts directly impact the company's performance.

108.     Participants in the corporation have a joint interest in building its competitive advantage and improving its performance. In this perspective, the role of corporate governance is to create a contractual framework that maximises the total returns of the corporation by improving the abilities, incentives and efforts of the corporation's resource providers.

109.     Admittedly, aligning interests is a complex and difficult task. Each society and company functions in a unique legal and cultural setting that dictates the parameters of the contracts that support relations among the parties. While explicit legal rules apply to corporate relationships, the culture also imbues the parties' relationships with certain "implicit" understandings.

110.     However, legal rules and cultural understandings should not restrict flexibility in aligning the interests of shareholders and other stakeholders. Undue restrictions may undermine entrepreneurship and negatively affect corporate performance and wealth creation.

> *"The United States would never have the high-technology business it has today if it wasn't for stock options. Many of these companies can not afford the cash outlay that is required to be able to attract the kind of management and the kind of skills that are needed. The solution for them is to make use of stock options."*
>
> Mr. Lawrence Weinbach, Chairman, President and Chief Executive Officer, Unisys Corp. (United States)

## 6.1    Contracting with Resource Providers

111.    Corporate performance is a function of teamwork. Selecting and motivating management, key professionals, employees and other resource providers is critical to corporate performance. As to managers, key professionals and employees, incentive compensation is an important tool for attracting and motivating capable corporate contributors. Performance-based compensation can be used to align these contributors' interests with shareholders' interest in successful corporate performance. This interest-alignment tool has enabled many companies to encourage entrepreneurial commitment to the success of the company.

◊    *Aligning the interests of management:* The Advisory Group believes that performance-based compensation that incorporates stock or stock options is most effective when implemented with consideration of three factors:

- The duration and exercise of management stock options should be related to the time frame in which corporate performance is to be measured. The appropriate time frame depends on industry and company circumstances, and the performance expected of managers.

- To eliminate the impact of overall market cycles on executive incomes, it is advisable to benchmark company performances to peer companies or peer company indices.

- Stock-based (and other) management compensation should be awarded with consideration of its relation to the compensation of lower-level employees. Remuneration gaps in the enterprise should reflect, and be perceived as reflecting, differentials in the market value of particular skills, experience and contributions to the success of the corporation.

◊ *Aligning the interests of key professionals:* Incentive compensation linked to performance goals can also be used to encourage key professionals to achieve specific objectives. For example, companies can reward scientists and engineers for achieving targeted technological advances. Performance measures that acknowledge specific objectives help align the interests of key personnel with a company's strategic objectives.

◊ *Aligning the interests of employees:* A company's general workforce is a major factor in corporate performance. Wages, benefits and other employee rights are determined through complex negotiated arrangements and understandings. Institutional factors beyond the scope of the individual company, such as corporate law, employment regulations, collective bargaining and employee representation practices, also play an important role. Nonetheless, each company has some flexibility, including via workers' councils and participation on supervisory boards, to determine the terms of its contracts with employees. Employee interests can be aligned with corporate performance through stock-based incentive compensation, including employee stock and option plans. Other incentives include work flexibility, training and performance-related remuneration systems. Designing such incentives is an area in which the board of directors can play an important role. Employment security is an issue that may pose a special challenge in corporate and national cultures that traditionally have viewed the employment relationship as relatively stable and permanent.

◊ *Aligning the interests of suppliers and customers:* The corporate interest is best aligned with the interests of its customers through the delivery of quality products and services at a fair price. Likewise, the corporate interest is best aligned with the interests of its suppliers by paying a fair price for their products and services.

## 6.2    The Role of the Board

112.    The board of directors is responsible for the adoption of incentives that adequately position the corporation to maximise corporate wealth. Independent (non-executive) members of the board have a special responsibility in ensuring that remuneration and incentives are appropriate and perceived as fair. Boards can learn from the domestic and international experiences of other companies in creating appropriate incentive systems.

> *"The problem with executive compensation is not necessarily the level of pay, but rather the fact that executives decide on it themselves."*
>
> Mr. Robert A.G. Monks, Principal, LENS Inc. (United States)

113.    In creating incentives, a board should consider the expectations of the various resource providers, the strategic objectives to be met, and the impact of corporate actions on the unique cultural and institutional setting in which the corporation operates, in both its domestic and its global operations.

• • •

114.    The Advisory Group believes that the role of the board of directors (comprised of at least some non-management members capable of independent judgement) in promoting competitive corporate performance through active oversight, including the creation of appropriate incentives, is an important area for further OECD study.

115.    The Advisory Group believes that further inquiry concerning company and board efforts to align the interests of managers, employees and shareholders, through performance-based compensation and other incentive schemes, may be useful.

## EXECUTIVE AND DIRECTOR COMPENSATION DISCLOSURE

*In the United Kingdom and the United States, disclosure of executive and director compensation to shareholders has gained attention:*

• The remuneration committee should make a report each year to the shareholders on behalf of the Board. The report should form part of, or be annexed to, the company's Annual Report and Accounts. It should be the main vehicle through which the company accounts to shareholders for Directors' remuneration.

• The report should set out the Company's policy on executive remuneration including levels, comparator groups of companies, individual components, performance criteria and measurement, pension provision, contracts of service and compensation commitments on early termination.

• The report should also include full details of all elements in the remuneration package of each individual Director by name, such as basic salary, benefits in kind, annual bonuses and long-term incentive schemes including share options.

*Directors' Remuneration: Report of a Study Group chaired by Sir Richard Greenbury,* at B1, B2 and B4 (July 1995) *(Greenbury Report).*

• In 1992, the US Securities and Exchange Commission revised its executive compensation disclosure rules to require comprehensive, factual disclosure of pay to top executives. The SEC rules require each board's compensation committee (or the full board, if the company does not maintain a compensation committee) to provide annually an explanation of its executive pay philosophy and its pay awards to the CEO for the previous year. In addition, the SEC rules require that the value of all forms of compensation awarded annually to top executives be disclosed in tabular form. A summary compensation table discloses the value of all forms of annual and long-term awards, including salary, cash bonuses, and stock awards, for the five most highly compensated executives, including the CEO. Another table contains additional information about the value of stock option grants and other stock-based awards for top executives. The SEC left untouched any pay disclosure requirements for directors... The Commission recommends that disclosure of director pay be consistent with disclosure of executive pay.

*Report of the National Association of Corporate Directors Commission on Director Compensation,* pp. 19-20 (1995).

## EMPLOYEE OWNERSHIP

*Employee share ownership provides a means to align employee and shareholder interests, reward performance, and recruit and retain personnel.*

- National Westminster Bank Plc. (UK) with 71 000 employees has been running employee shareholder and profit sharing plans since 1979. The company estimates that about 4 per cent of its share capital is owned by employees. The company cites the main advantages of employee ownership as a way to:

  - promote employee savings;
  - motivate, recruit and retain employees;
  - align employee and shareholder interests;
  - improve employee awareness of the financial performance of the company;
  - provide employees with the opportunity to take advantage of tax breaks;
  - reward performance;
  - enhance remuneration packages.

- Ciment Lafarge, a French company with 35 000 employees in approximately 40 countries, launched an employee share ownership programme in 1995, to which 15 000 employees have since subscribed – representing 1.3 per cent of outstanding equity. Although in some countries the policy has met legal restrictions or resistance from local shareholders, Lafarge believes that the employee share ownership plan is a significant factor in promoting a cohesive workforce throughout many different countries.

*Source:* FONDACT, Member of International Association for Financial Participation.

# CHAPTER 7. RECOGNISING SOCIETAL INTERESTS

*Companies do not act independently from the societies in which they operate. Accordingly, corporate actions must be compatible with societal objectives concerning social cohesion, individual welfare and equal opportunities for all. Attending to legitimate social concerns should, in the long run, benefit all parties, including investors. At times, however, there may be a trade-off between short-term social costs and the long-term benefits to society of having a healthy, competitive private sector. Societal needs that transcend the responsive ability of the private sector should be met by specific public policy measures, rather than by impeding improvements in corporate governance and capital allocation.*

116.    Corporations are dependent on the societies in which they operate. As members of society, corporations benefit from, and must abide by, society's laws, regulations and broader collective objectives. In turn, the societies in which corporations operate benefit both economically and socially from corporations' commercial activities.

117.    Global competition in the markets for goods, services and capital exerts pressures for improved corporate performance, which pressures in turn can impact corporate relationships with local communities and resource providers; this can give rise to social tensions. For example, in competitive product, service and capital markets, a corporation may face the need to reduce its workforce. At times, accepting such short-term social costs may be necessary to achieve the long-term benefits to society of building a competitive corporation and, ultimately, a healthy, competitive private sector. Moreover, corporations that find it socially difficult to reduce their workforce when necessary will likely be more conservative in increasing their workforce.

> *"Relationships with stakeholders have been changing for quite some time in the manufacturing industry. Changing technologies and global competition require companies to seek greater and greater flexibility and the traditional social contracts may conflict with this objective."*
>
> Ms. Heidi Kunz, Chief Financial Officer, ITT Industries (United States)

118.    The Advisory Group believes that societal concerns about corporate responses to market pressures are legitimate. Attending to social concerns may benefit all parties, including investors, and is a matter of business judgement. Efforts should be made to clarify that capitalising on market opportunities to assure long-term corporate success is the primary reason to promote improved corporate governance, and that good governance should accommodate societal concerns to the extent possible. With this understanding, adequate private sector and, when necessary, governmental responses can be formulated.

119.    The Advisory Group believes that corporate boards have an important role in the corporation's efforts to balance the interests of economic efficiency and society's broader objectives.

> *"To me there are two fundamental responsibilities for the board. One is accountability, and the other is direction of the business. No company can operate without proper regard to all its relevant stakeholders. That is a fundamental responsibility of management supervised by the board of directors. The board can in fact set the climate for these relationships with stakeholders."*
>
> Sir Ronald Hampel, Chairman ICI and Chairman of the Committee on Corporate Governance (United Kingdom)

120.    It is the Advisory Group's view that when significant tensions between improved corporate economic performance and societal needs and objectives arise, such that they cannot be accommodated by the corporate sector on a voluntary basis, those tensions should be addressed by specific public-policy measures, rather than by impeding improvements in corporate governance and capital allocation.

- A company must develop relationships relevant to its success. These will depend on the nature of the company's business; but they will include those with employees, customers, suppliers, credit providers, local communities and governments. It is management's responsibility to develop policies which address these matters; in doing so they must have regard to the overriding objective of preserving and enhancing the shareholders' investment over time. The board's task is to approve appropriate policies and to monitor the performance of management in implementing them.

- As regards stakeholders, different types of companies will have different relationships, and directors can meet their legal duties to shareholders, and can pursue the objective of long-term shareholder value successfully, only by developing and sustaining these stakeholder relationships. We believe that shareholders recognise that it is in their best interests for companies to do this and – increasingly – to have regard to the broader public acceptability of their conduct.

*Final Report of the Hampel Committee on Corporate Governance*, at 1.16 and 1.18 (January 1998).

121.    The Advisory Group recognises that accommodating the need for improved corporate performance and societal interests is complex, and identifies five related groups of issues that may impact corporate accommodation of societal interests:

◊    corporate trust bases;

◊    potential income and opportunity path divergence;

◊    investments with high social and low economic returns;

◊    privatisation; and

◊    corporate citizenship.

## 7.1    Corporate Trust Bases

122.    Corporations are sometimes viewed as "communities" of resource providers (owners, managers, employees, suppliers, customers, local communities, etc.) that have a "trust base" founded on long-standing commitments and expectations. The social and economic value of a

corporation's "trust base" depends on the individual corporation and the values of the society in which it functions.

123.    In the new competitive environment, the corporate need to quickly shift activities to new or improved products and technologies may be inconsistent with a company's long-term commitments to certain resource providers. At the same time, dynamic competitive circumstances also create new business opportunities for resource providers. Therefore, many resource providers also have an interest in more flexible business relationships.

124.    The Advisory Group recognises that in certain circumstances, efficiency gains from a corporation's long-standing commitments may prove superior to shorter-term, more flexible and more formal relationships with resource providers. However, in global markets, corporations must compete with entities that may have a different balance of social and economic values. Tensions between the *social* and *economic* value of long-term commitments may become particularly visible in those enterprises, sectors and countries where long-term commitments among corporate participants are highly valued. When such societies seek to promote the ability of their corporations to compete globally, special consideration may need to be given to the pace and collective costs of the necessary cultural adjustments.

125.    The Advisory Group also recognises that in competitive global capital markets, most investors are focused on economic profitability. Foregoing investment returns for broader collective objectives that are not fully compatible with economic efficiency may be contrary to certain investors' objectives. For example, institutional investors have fiduciary responsibilities to their large numbers of beneficiaries (who are, in turn, a large and growing share of the "public"), which may preclude them from supporting corporate efforts aimed at certain non-economic goals.

126.    As previously stated, when significant tensions develop between economic efficiency and the social value of long-standing corporate commitments, the society's broader collective interest may have to be addressed by the government. However, it should be recognised that governmental action may entail costs to enterprises as well as to the broader society due to global competition.

## 7.2    Potential Income and Opportunity Path Divergence

127.    A corollary to efficient capital allocation is improvement in the efficiency of the resource markets: corporations' contracts with resource providers are today less bundled, standardised and uniformly structured than in the past. With respect to labour, reward mechanisms tend to recognise genuine contributions and career paths tend to be settled according to individual abilities. In this context, less efficient market participants may lose traditional benefits from implicit cross-subsidies, income transfers and mutual insurance mechanisms within and between corporations.

128.    While the Advisory Group recognises the legitimacy of societal concerns about the impact of market forces on individuals, and on income gaps and divergent opportunity paths, it believes that more efficient capital allocation and improved corporate governance should improve the total income and employment level of a society over the long term, thereby helping to create additional resources for more effective corporate and societal responses.

129.    The Advisory Group also notes that individual companies can and do respond on a voluntary basis to perceived inequities. Such voluntary initiatives range from compensation programmes that link employee remuneration to corporate performance, to the retraining of undervalued employees.

130.    The corporate board is responsible for ensuring that corporate practices involving the treatment of resource providers are perceived as fair. A board committee that is charged with reviewing the entire remuneration structure of the corporation may be useful.

## 7.3    Effective Disclosure of Contractual and Governance Structures

131.    The disclosure of the corporation's contractual and governance structures may reduce uncertainties for investors and help lower capital costs by decreasing related risk premia. Such transparency may also encourage a common understanding of the "rules of the game," and provide employees with information that may help reduce labour friction.

132.    Voluntary dissemination of a company's codes of conduct, governance guidelines or other formal or informal policies may be used to disclose more information about the corporation's internal and governance-related relationships and structures.

## 7.4    Investments with High Social and Low Economic Returns

133.    Pressures for efficient capital allocation and corporate performance may reduce investments in programmes and enterprises that are perceived as having high social but low economic returns, such as adopting environmentally friendly technologies and undertaking research projects having long payout periods, supporting training activities that benefit apprentices who may not join the corporation, and diversifying geographic investment to benefit local communities despite low returns. While this is the rational outcome of corporations' need to reward investors, the economic benefits of such programmes – frequently in the long term – should not be undervalued. For example, such programmes can have a major impact on corporate reputation, which for many enterprises is critically important.

134.    For example, many investors recognise that it is in the corporation's economic interest to enhance public credibility by engaging in charitable activity. Examples include: charitable contributions to local community programmes and non-profit organisations, and company-supported volunteer activities. Such activities impact the asset-value of the corporation's reputation (although the asset enhancement may be an intangible). Indeed, some corporations have found that a strong commitment to social responsibility serves to differentiate them from competitors, and thus is a source of competitive advantage in marketing and in hiring. Corporate boards should be responsible for these "corporate citizenship" issues, and their decisions and priorities in this area should be disclosed to investors.

135.    Similarly, if properly structured, research and training efforts may have justifiable long-term economic benefits. Regulation and contractual safeguards – such as intellectual property protection rules and non-competition agreements with trained employees – may assist in capturing these benefits. Active board participation in structuring such programmes may diminish perceived risks of investment in socially beneficial activities.

136.    As to activities that do not promise a corporate benefit over some acceptable time period, there still may be some investors willing to devote resources to carry on high social return activities. For example, some institutional investors affiliated with religious organisations may consider social benefits in their investment decisions. Full disclosure of high social return activities by corporations may serve to attract those investors.

137.    To the extent that gaps remain between desired social outcomes and those projects that can be justified through a promise of economic returns over

some acceptable time frame, the use of traditional public-policy tools may be used to encourage the social outcome desired. Devices such as R&D tax credits, training incentives and location incentives for businesses in economically distressed areas are currently used by most, if not all, OECD countries for this purpose.

## 7.5    Privatisation

138.    A number of OECD economies are transferring or considering transferring ownership of companies from public authorities to private investors. Such transfers impact the economic objectives, organisational design, investment decisions, service mixes, pricing policies, etc., of the newly privatised companies, and gain social importance in those enterprises which, prior to their privatisation, fulfilled significant social functions, through their pricing, service, regional investment and employment policies.

139.    If such functions are perceived by significant segments of society as contributing to collective welfare, their fate after privatisation may become an issue. As public opinions are better informed about the impact of competition in global markets on social objectives – either in terms of these objectives' possible pursuit through alternative policy means, or being better substituted by market mechanisms and outcomes – privatisations could proceed under stronger social consensus and political stability.

## 7.6    Corporate Citizenship

140.    Clearly, as members of society, corporations are expected to abide by the laws and regulations of the countries in which they operate. However, corporate citizenship extends beyond technical compliance with law to a sensitivity to the broader collective objectives of the societies in which corporations operate.

141.    In the global economy, sensitivity to the many societies in which an individual corporation may operate can pose a challenge. Increasingly, however, investors in international capital markets expect corporations to forego certain activities – such as use of child or prison labour, bribery, support of oppressive regimes, and environmental disruption – even when those activities may not be expressly prohibited in a particular jurisdiction in which the corporation operates.

142.    In addition to foregoing activities that are viewed as harmful to broader collective objectives, depending on the society, corporations may also be expected to engage actively in socially responsible conduct. Examples include: providing employees with access to health care, retirement benefits or day care; maintaining a drug-free workplace; encouraging diversity of race and gender in the corporation and in the corporation's suppliers; supporting the education of future potential employees; and adopting environmentally friendly technologies.

143.    In accommodating the expectations of society, corporations must not lose sight of the primary corporate objective, which is to generate long-term economic profit to enhance shareholder (or investor) value. The Advisory Group recognises that, over the long term, acting as a responsible corporate citizen is consistent with this economic objective.

---

### VOLUNTARY INTERNATIONAL STANDARDS

*The voluntary adoption of certifiable international standards provides corporations with a means of demonstrating a commitment to socially acceptable practices.*

Based on International Labour Organization conventions, the Universal Declaration on Human Rights and the United Nations Convention on the Rights of the Child, Social Accountability 8000 is designed to provide a common framework for ethical production and sourcing by companies doing business throughout the world. The standard sets forth basic minimum requirements relating to, among other things, the use of child and forced labour, worker health and safety, trade union rights, discriminatory practices, maximum working hours and minimum compensation.

Companies that adhere to SA 8000 can apply for certification under the standard, which then enables the certified company to advertise conformance to the standard. Certified companies will be audited periodically by an independent auditor to ensure that the standard is in fact being met.

The standard was released for discussion in October 1997 by a non-profit think-tank – the US- and UK-based Council on Economic Priorities Accreditation Agency. Participating companies include Avon, Otto-Versand and Toys R Us.

*Source:* Council on Economic Priorities Accreditation Agency.

●  ●  ●

144.    The Advisory Group believes that further inquiry may be useful concerning:

◊   the impact of corporate investment in areas of potential high social – but low short-term private economic – return on the primary corporate objective of generating long-term economic gain, and the potential value of disclosing such information; and

◊   the impact on corporate governance practices of privatising government-owned enterprises.

# DISCLOSURE OF CORPORATE POLICIES:
## The Case of Environmental Standards

## OMRON Corporation

*OMRON Corporation's Environmental Charter and Policy is disclosed to shareholders in the Annual Report, and expressly recognises a broad responsibility to society as a whole:*

- Our corporate policy holds that as a responsible corporation, OMRON should contribute to the betterment of customers as well as society as a whole and the environment. Our environmental charter and policy were created to help prevent the further pollution of the environment as well as to reduce current levels. Guided by this policy and charter, we are working together as a corporate group to develop environment-friendly products, reduce the burden placed on the environment by our production and distribution activities, and conduct environmental audits to ensure the continued progress of our efforts... Aiming for harmony between the environment and mankind, we will use environment-friendly technology and responsible corporate activities to contribute to a better world.

*OMRON Corporation Environmental Charter and Policy, Annual Report, pp. 11-12 (1997).*

## Salomon Inc.

*The Environmental Policy Statement of Salomon Inc. expresses a similar recognition of broad social responsibility with respect to environmental protection and emphasizes the role of the board of directors:*

- Salomon Inc is committed to protection of the environment and the health and safety of our employees and the communities in which we conduct our business. We recognise that environmental protection is one of the most important issues affecting businesses today... [I]t is the policy of Salomon to endeavour to...

  - Objectively evaluate our environmental performance and identify areas for improvement. Pertinent performance review information will be provided on a regular basis to the Board of Directors through the Environmental Committee.

  - Provide the Board of Directors information about environmental matters that the Board needs to perform its responsibilities, and make required information about environmental matters available to shareholders, employees, the authorities and the public.

*Salomon Inc. Environmental Policy Statement (3 June 1992).*

## ANNEX 1A

## REPORT FROM THE OECD BUSINESS SECTOR COLLOQUIUM ON CORPORATE GOVERNANCE

### Institutional Modernisation for Effective and Adaptive Corporate Governance

### 1.    Background

On 10-11 June 1997 the Industry Division of the DSTI organised, together with the OECD Business Sector Advisory Group on Corporate Governance, a one-and-a-half-day colloquium on corporate governance. The event, which took place at the OECD headquarters in Paris, welcomed around 130 participants from both the private and the public sectors.

The prime purpose of the Colloquium was to give the Business Sector Advisory Group an opportunity to consult with a wider circle of distinguished business executives from North America, Europe and Japan on the progress made in their work. It was an occasion to discuss some of the Advisory Group's tentative positions and the direction of their future work. It also provided a forum for invited panellists and other participants to present their views and exchange experiences in relation to the issues raised.

To stimulate discussion and facilitate the search for a coherent perspective, all panellists had been provided with a background document prepared by the Secretariat under the supervision of the Business Sector Advisory Group. The central element in the background document was a description of the current challenges in the area of capital allocation and corporate governance. All panellists were invited to comment on the accuracy and implications of this analysis.

In addition to comments on general developments, panellists were given the opportunity to comment on a set of selected topics where changes in corporate governance have put current economic practices, legal doctrines and social understandings under scrutiny. The selected topics were: *i)* The Mission of the Corporation and the Role of Investors; *ii)* The New Role of the Board of Directors; *iii)* New Needs for Information; *iv)* New Contracting Practices Between Investors and Corporations.

## 2.　　Discussions on the Selected Topics

### *i)*　　*The Mission of the Corporation and the Role of Investors*

The opening session, devoted to the mission of the corporation and the role of investors, provided an opportunity for panellists with experience from different cultural and historical contexts to discuss how new economic circumstances may affect the perception of the business corporation's role in society. It was generally agreed that the successful long-term running of a company requires proper attention to all its resource providers, including suppliers of financial and human capital, input products and services, technology, etc. From this point of departure, the discussion focused on how these concerns about the overall outcome are best met in an increasingly competitive world with globally mobile capital.

Several panellists argued that maximising profits was the most efficient way of serving the wider interests of all stakeholders and resource providers. A close and continuous concern with financial results will highlight the need for competitiveness, make the process of corporate restructuring smoother and avoid unnecessarily abrupt and painful adjustments. From this perspective, the expectations of society at large and of individual stakeholders should be aligned with the company's overriding objective to maximise profits in a competitive environment. It was also noted that this attitude does not exclude the company entering into sophisticated and sometimes far-reaching profit-sharing arrangements and other incentive programmes with critical resource providers other than shareholders. As a matter of fact, the ability to remunerate resource providers in accordance with their unique contributions to the overriding objective of maximising profits could be seen as key ingredient for corporate success.

While recognising the special role of residual claimants, panellists also discussed the fact that many companies pursue goals other than maximising returns to shareholders. Companies or managers that are willing to forego profitable business opportunities if they conflict with other performance criteria, including labour relations or environmental concerns, were mentioned

78

as examples of such behaviour. When such objectives are pursued unilaterally by a company and at the explicit potential expense of shareholders' income, it was questioned whether such behaviour would gain long-term acceptance in the investment community. Examples were also given of times when the mere possibility of introducing such alternative goals had discouraged investors. However, examples of successful companies pursuing "alternative" objectives were also presented, and explicit reference was made to the cosmetics company, The Body Shop. There seemed to be general agreement that corporate objectives other than maximising profits should be considered as perfectly legitimate as long as they are clearly defined and fully disclosed to investors.

Attention was also given to the need for social acceptance when modifying certain established corporate governance practices. If such acceptance is not at hand, it may prove difficult to pursue reforms that will enhance long-term corporate efficiency and economic performance. Special reference was made to public opinion in relation to take-overs and performance-related remuneration systems for management.

As for the role of investors, it was generally agreed that it was useful to make a distinction between two main types of corporate governance strategies (*i.e.* arm's length and relational investors) as they illustrate different ways of assessing and monitoring management performance. It was also recognised that the two strategies may require different routines and instruments for communicating with management and monitoring company performance. In the case of the arm's length strategy one panellist suggested that corporate governance concerns were best dealt with by concentrating on the functioning of the board of directors. One large diversified investor pointed out that its ability to advise its more than 1 000 portfolio companies on distinct company matters was very limited. Another large pension fund characterised its strategy as one of requiring that management subscribe to a few basic corporate governance principles in exchange for the fund's long-term engagement in the company. Communicating this policy to the company was seen as an important manifestation of the investor's ambition to create mutual trust and commitment.

In the case of relational and active investing, it was suggested that more customised and direct ways of evaluating and monitoring company performance are often necessary. As important elements for achieving this, panellists mentioned the possibility to be represented on the board of directors, direct involvement in the selection and appointment of the management team, careful design of distinct incentive systems and in certain instances a readiness (and ability) by the investor to participate in the day-to-day running of the company.

## ii)      The New Role of the Board of Directors

In discussing the role of the board of directors it was widely recognised that it has a key role in supervising management on behalf of the shareholders and in formulating the strategic direction of the company. One participant summarised this as "accountability and direction". This recognition of the board's central role in corporate governance was then contrasted with the often remarkable lack of explicit formulation and general awareness of the board's work methods and the specific tasks of its directors. Such omission, when resulting in passive and uninformed boards, can severely hamper the company's ability to restructure and set out new strategic directions.

The point was made that the process of formulating work methods and objectives for the board must be generated at company level. How a company's board should organise its day-to-day work should not be mandated by any outside authority, but instead should be clarified within the company through a process of self-evaluation and assessment. Panellists gave examples of the possible elements of such internal board guidelines including a mission statement and the formulation of evaluation methods. A participant with particular experience in the field suggested that key elements in the process of creating a more proactive board were to include non-management directors and to make everyone on the board aware of what is expected from them.

One participant reminded the meeting that the functioning of the board depends on the quality of its members and their ability to carry out some tasks better than management. It was suggested that the comparative advantages of the board as a distinct company organ are to select the management team, decide on large investments/acquisitions and act in times of corporate crisis. These comparative advantages of the board should be kept in mind when designing the work methods of the board and its composition. In relation to individual board members' abilities to carry out their tasks properly, some panellists expressed concern about the number of boards on which some directors were represented. In order to participate in the work of a proactive board, directors need to set aside sufficient time, which should imply a natural limit to the number of boards on which they can sit.

*iii)*     ***New Needs for Information***

Concerning the role of information, there was broad consensus among panellists that the quantity and quality of information available to the investment community is of key importance to efficient capital allocation and good corporate governance. In order for information to play this role it needs to be accurate and relevant. Constant work is therefore required to adjust and improve corporate reporting to new circumstances. As a way to make information more complete, special mention was made of attempts to disclose, in standardised form, different kinds of non-financial information.

From the active investor's point of view it was stated, however, that although useful and important, publicly available information, be it financial or non-financial, is only a starting point. For their long-term involvement and ability to contribute positively to company decisions, active investors need, and will constantly seek, additional information. Such information should provide the ability to assess not only the historical value of whatever assets the company may possess, but also more customised information about the future earnings potential of these assets. In many circumstances, the ability to access, process and communicate such information is limited to those investors who are willing (and able) to take on an insider status, foregoing liquidity in the company's stock.

Hence, from a corporate governance point of view, it is not only the content or frequency of information that is of importance. Equally significant are the ways in which information can be communicated and capitalised by those who invest in generating unique information about the company's future prospects. One panellist formulated it as the right of those who make an extra effort in informing themselves about a company to be able to gain a market advantage.

From this perspective, one panellist argued that under a proper legal framework, it may be efficient to pursue two complementary avenues for meeting different investors' needs for information. This would involve both improvements in the quality of public information and improvements in communicating strategic, sensitive and confidential information to certain owners holding relational stakes in the company.

*iv)*    ***New Contracting Practices Between Investors and Corporations***

The presence at the Colloquium of companies and investors with varying strategies and experience from operating under different competitive circumstances provided a fruitful basis for discussing the possibilities for developing more efficient corporate governance practices. There was general agreement that a key prerequisite for progress in this area was the ability to shape and implement the appropriate contractual arrangements between investors and between investors and the company. This will include several aspects of stakeholder interactions and for this reason, the session on new contracting practices was seen as pulling together many of the issues discussed in earlier sessions.

It was stated that many companies and investors today are facing a growing complexity of agency, incentive and information issues and will in the future become increasingly sophisticated in corporate governance. This was especially underlined by some of the panellists from countries with a hitherto less-widespread debate in the field.

Several panellists agreed that it would be beneficial to explicitly recognise the distinct contributions from liquid placements by fully diversified investors on the one hand, and actively involved relational investors with significant stakes on the other hand. The two types of investors were generally seen as complementary and can contribute in different ways to the monitoring of companies.

From the perspective of a pension fund, one panellist suggested that the different contracts that may be demanded by different kinds of investors may manifest themselves in different investment instruments reflecting different return requirements and information needs.

The need to develop and refine contractual structures that will improve corporate governance was also discussed in relation to the specific circumstances in certain industries such as the high-tech industry and the service industry, where more than traditional outside control is often required for exerting efficient corporate governance. The size of the firm was also mentioned as a factor to consider when designing contractual structures and legal forms. One example held to be promising in this respect was the introduction in Germany of the Kommanditgesellschaft auf Aktien (KGaA) that according to one panellist has the potential to solve many of the corporate governance problems in smaller and medium-sized companies.

## 3.　　Main Conclusions

Participants to the Colloquium and the Business Sector Advisory Group Members concluded the Colloquium with a strong sense of common achievement. A much-needed common international language and framework to address the different aspects of the current corporate governance agenda took shape. Participants expressed confidence in the major orientation of the work presented to them and recognition was given to the OECD as a leading catalyst in this area of structural adjustment.

The discussions during the Colloquium provided input both to the immediate task of the Advisory Group in preparing their report to the Organisation, and to the more general task of developing the overall OECD work in this field.

The Chairman of the Advisory Group tentatively summarised the discussions in a number of key areas with potential bearing on the direction and content of the Group's work:

◊　As regulatory barriers between national economies fall and global competition for capital increases, investment capital will follow the path to those corporations that have adopted efficient governance standards, which include acceptable accounting and disclosure standards, satisfactory investor protections and board practices designed to provide independent, accountable oversight of managers.

◊　Philosophical differences about the corporation's mission continue, although views appear to be converging. For example, in the United States it is increasingly accepted that the goal of maximising shareholder returns over the long term requires responsiveness to the demands and expectations of other stakeholders, while in Japan and Germany, there is growing recognition that profit maximising strategies can – in the long term – be consonant with societal interests in a strong economy and low unemployment.

◊　So long as there is adequate disclosure such that "the market can decide", corporations can diverge from the goal of maximising shareholder interests. In other words, return on investment can be tempered by another goal if all investors are properly informed when they purchase stock. For example, a company could say, "our goal is to secure jobs for our employees, even if that means at times foregoing profits" or "we take special care to protect the environment, avoid harm to animals and promote the interests of workers in underdeveloped nations, even if that may lower our potential profit on a product" – as is the case for The Body Shop. Investors are then free to invest, knowing that their interests are not exclusive – and the market can decide whether other goals are important to investors.

◊ Regulations that impede market-based solutions to corporate governance should be avoided. In a global market, while regulations are required to protect shareholders against fraud and self-dealing by the corporation's directors and managers and to ensure adequate disclosure of information, regulation as to board practices and the internal management of the corporation is more likely to create barriers to innovation and adaptability than to provide any real benefit.

◊ It was recognised that differences in the character of corporations, together with variations in the specific competencies and strategies of investors, may justify differences in corporate governance practices. Taking particular incentive, agency and information aspects of individual corporations into consideration, properly designed and "customised" governance designs can serve an important function in improving monitoring and decreasing capital costs.

◊ While regulation is not appropriate, there was strong consensus that there needs to be a global understanding of "the rules of the game". Issues of board practice and internal management should be subject to voluntary adaptation and evolution, in an environment of globally understood minimum standards of acceptable practice.

◊ A common, universal set of accounting standards would be beneficial.

Viewed in an OECD context, the Colloquium confirmed the clear link between corporate governance and the Organisation's structural policy agenda aiming at stimulating entrepreneurship, productivity, growth and employment creation in Member economies. For this reason, the following observations and conclusions from the Colloquium may constitute particularly relevant elements when further developing OECD's work in this area.

◊ The general experience of panellists was that business enterprises have to remunerate their capital at an increasingly similar market price. The risk-adjusted returns required by domestic and international investors, from enterprises of all sizes, types, sectors and countries, converge. New standards apply both to funds provided by financial intermediaries (including, increasingly, pension funds) and cash flows generated and reinvested within enterprises.

*Under such circumstances, macro- and micro-level growth policies cannot assume in the future that capital resources may be remunerated consistently at below market prices – i.e. as sheltered and captive resources.*

◊ Competition in the financial sector has given financial intermediaries hitherto non-existent incentives to proactively identify the most promising and rapidly growing business investment areas. Equity placements sharing the risks and returns of business corporations of all types, sizes, sectors and countries tend to increase.

*There was general agreement that this development opens new opportunities and new avenues for the funding of entrepreneurial activities, in two forms:*

*i) within existing firms (in the form of long-term projects with a high intangible content, for which equity funds are important, such as new product development, R&D, marketing, overseas investments, new capacity creation, etc.); and*

*ii) by supporting the creation of new enterprises (as pure start-ups, as spin-offs from large organisations, or as new concerns resulting from privatisations).*

◊ Present developments create a strong common interest between investors, entrepreneurs, managers, the workforce, pension beneficiaries, local communities and policy makers (as the trustees of the public interest) in improving the capability of the economy to direct capital resources to their most promising and productive uses. To monitor the efficient application of capital resources in their intended uses is part of the same function.

*From this perspective, improved capital allocation and corporate governance should not be seen as a zero-sum game between investors and other stakeholders in enterprises. When deployed in its productive form, it is a positive-sum process of activity, wealth and employment generation with congruent interests between parties.*

◊ Present developments in corporate governance and capital markets are sometimes coupled with transition problems, for example in terms of employment adjustments, as an outcome of rapid (or long-delayed) improvements in capital allocation and corporate governance. Such improvements may also create resource allocation sub-optimalities when social *vs.* private returns of investments happen to differ significantly (for example in certain areas of R&D, employee training, investments in declining regions, etc.). This relates more generally to the "social capital" issue which raises collective action problems.

> *The conclusion, however, was that these problems should be addressed by specific policy tools, rather than by hindering improvements in capital allocation and corporate governance. In this context, voluntary decisions by individual companies to pursue non-profit-maximising objectives should also be acknowledged as long as this is done in a transparent fashion disclosing the company's alternative objectives.*

◊ In the important process of improving and strengthening the capital allocation and corporate governance infrastructure of the economy, two principal tasks for policy makers were identified during the Colloquium. The first task was stressed more frequently, but the importance of the second was also mentioned:

> *i)* The regulatory reform agenda: *Reviewing and reforming public regulations which may adversely affect the establishment of entrepreneurial and wealth-creating relationships between investors, entrepreneurs and managers. Constraints on the types of investments permitted to pension funds, restrictive rules concerning the disclosure of forward-looking information by companies, tax biases between various financing instruments such as debt and equity instruments are examples.*

> *ii)* The institutional improvement agenda: *Creating a legal/institutional infrastructure that facilitates the adoption of more efficient investment strategies, instruments and contracts in the new economic environment. This is effected via public provisions that support contracting arrangements between parties, such as corporation forms available in corporate law, information disclosure formats prescribed by accounting rules, investment vehicles and contracts covered and serviced by securities regulations, etc. In the new economic environment, innovations and adjustments may be needed in these areas in order to provide the framework for innovative private practices.*

◊ Panellists agreed that OECD countries face current challenges from different domestic points of departure. Prevailing business traditions and practices, familiar business incorporation forms, expertise of local investors with specific investment vehicles, the level of legal services easing transactions between investors and corporations, the range of stock exchange services available, and society's political expectations as to the principles of capital allocation and corporate governance – and the resulting stance of public policies – all differ.

But equally widespread was the opinion that all modern economies share the same task of facilitating positive-sum interactions between financial investors on the one hand (with their globally converging financial objectives and strategies), and entrepreneurs and enterprises on the other hand (with their globally converging business opportunities and risks).

> *The general conclusion from this discussion was that the practical corporate governance agenda in different countries is converging in many vital areas, although historical and cultural differences will continue to exist.*

◊   It was fully recognised that present developments create increasing room for mutual learning. Such exchange of experiences and opinions takes place between companies, between investors, between governments and between other regulators – indeed between all parties having a practical interest and responsibility in strengthening the capital allocation and corporate governance basis of the economy.

> *It was concluded from this understanding that improvements in practices by mutual learning could be enhanced by "guidelines" or "references" in various areas of corporate governance. Such guidance would screen, review and communicate successful experiences, but should not be viewed as statutory or regulatory tools to mandate or legislate specific governance designs.*

> *Such points of reference for improved corporate governance will have both private practice and public policy elements, and may respond to increasing demands not only from OECD economies, but also from transition and developing countries.*

**ANNEX 1B**

# OECD BUSINESS SECTOR COLLOQUIUM ON CORPORATE GOVERNANCE: PROGRAMME

## *DAY 1: 10 JUNE 1997*

*Opening of the Colloquium*: **Mr. Donald J. Johnston,** Secretary-General, OECD

*Welcome Address:* **Mr. Risaburo Nezu**, Director, OECD Directorate for Science, Technology and Industry (DSTI)

*Introductory Remarks*: **Mr. Ira M. Millstein**, Senior Partner, Weil, Gotshal & Manges, LLP, Chairman of the OECD Business Sector Advisory Group on Corporate Governance.

**SESSION 1: The Mission of the Business Corporation and the Role of Investors**

Panel:

**Ms. Heidi Kunz**, CFO, ITT Industries, United States

**Dr. Henning Schulte-Noelle**, Chairman of the Board of Management, Allianz AG, Germany

**Mr. Jean Saint-Geours**, Former Chairman, Commission des Opérations de Bourses, France

**Mr. Keikichi Honda**, Chairman and Representative Director, Nihon Sun Microsystems K.K., Japan

**Mr. Kimitoshi Hasegawa**, Managing Director, Dai-ichi Life Research Institute Inc., Japan

**Mr. Alastair Ross Goobey**, CEO, Hermes, United Kingdom

## SESSION 2: The New Role of the Board of Directors

Panel:

**Sir Ronald Hampel**, Chairman, ICI and Chairman, The Committee on Corporate Governance, United Kingdom

**Mr. Gérard Worms**, Président du Conseil des Commanditaires, Banque Rothschild et Compagnie Banque Paris, France

**Mr. Gregory H. Lau**, Executive Director, Executive Compensation and Corporate Governance, General Motors Corporation, United States

**Mr. Komei Kinoshita**, Auditor, Yamaichi Securities Co. Ltd., Japan

**Mr. Hervé de Carmoy**, Président du Conseil d'Administration de la Banque Industrielle et Mobilière Privée, France

## SESSION 3: New Needs for Information

Panel:

**Mr. Michel Pebereau**, Chairman and CEO, Banque Nationale de Paris, France

**Ms. Nancy B. Peretsman**, Managing Director, Allen & Company Inc., United States

**Mr. Toshihiro Kiribuchi**, Senior Corporate Advisor to the Board of Directors, OMRON Corporation, Japan

**Mr. Lawrence Weinbach**, Chairman and CEO, Andersen Worldwide, United States

**Mr. Nigel C.L. Macdonald**, Partner, Ernst & Young, United Kingdom

Reception hosted by The Swedish Corporate Governance Forum at the Château de la Muette, Room G. Marshall

## SESSION 4: New Contracting Practices between Investors and Corporations

Panel:

**Mr. Robert A.G. Monks**, Principal, LENS, United States

**Dr. Rolf-E. Breuer**, Spokesman of the Board, Deutsche Bank AG, Germany

**Mr. Woong Soon Song**, The General Counsel, Samsung Group, Korea

**Mr. Guy de Panafieu,** Vice-Président, Lyonnaise des Eaux, France

**Mr. Lennart Låftman**, Managing Director, Swedish National Pension Fund 5th Board, Sweden

**Dr. Bernhard Wunderlin**, Managing Director, Harald Quandt Holding GmbH, Germany

**Mr. Guy de Selliers**, Deputy Vice President, European Bank for Reconstruction and Development

**Mr. Joseph L. Rice III**, Chairman and CEO, Clayton, Dubilier & Rice Inc., United States

## SESSION 5: General Discussion and Summing up by the Advisory Group

Advisory Group Members:

**Mr. Michel Albert**, Membre du Conseil de la Politique Monétaire, Banque de France

**Sir Adrian Cadbury**, Former Chairman Cadbury-Schweppes and the Cadbury Commission on Financial Aspects of Corporate Governance

**Mr. Robert E. Denham**, CEO Salomon Inc.

**Dr. Dieter Feddersen**, Feddersen, Laule, Scherzberg & Ohle Hansen Ewerwahn

**Mr. Ira M. Millstein** (Chairman), Senior Partner, Weil, Gotshal & Manges, LLP

**Mr. Nobuo Tateisi**, Chairman, OMRON Corporation

Concluding Remark: **Ms. Joanna R. Shelton,** Deputy Secretary-General, OECD

# ANNEX 1C

## OECD BUSINESS SECTOR COLLOQUIUM ON CORPORATE GOVERNANCE: LIST OF PARTICIPANTS

| Surname | First name | Affiliation | Country |
|---------|-----------|-------------|---------|
| ALBERT | Michel | Membre du Conseil de la Politique Monétaire, Banque de France | France |
| ALEXANDER | Thomas | Director, Directorate for Education, Employment, Labour and Social Affairs, OECD | |
| ANDERSSON | Thomas | Deputy Director, Directorate for Science, Technology and Industry, OECD | |
| AVICE | Franck | Chargé de Mission, Ministère de l'Industrie, de la Poste et des Télécommunications | France |
| BATE | Steven | Executive Director, OECD Business and Industry Advisory Committee (BIAC) | |
| BIANCO | Magda | Bank of Italy | Italy |
| BIANCHI | Marcello | CONSOB (Bank Association) | Italy |
| BILGIC | Mehmet T. | Vice President, Karabük Kardemir Iron & Steel Corporation | Turkey |

93

| Surname | First name | Affiliation | Country |
|---------|-----------|-------------|---------|
| BLOMMESTEIN | Hendrikus | Principal Administrator, Financial Affairs Division, Directorate for Financial, Fiscal and Enterprise Affairs, OECD | |
| BONNIER | Karl-Adam | Chairman, Swedish Corporate Governance Forum | Sweden |
| BORE | Einar | Executive Officer, Ministry of Finance | Norway |
| BOTSCH | Andreas | Senior Policy Adviser, OECD Trade Union Advisory Committee (TUAC) | |
| BOULE | Suzanne | | United States |
| BOZ | Sevgi | Economic Counsellor, Permanent Delegation to the OECD | Turkey |
| BRANCATO | Carolyn | Director, Global Corporate Governance Research Center, The Conference Board | United States |
| BREUER | Rolf-E. | Spokesman of the Board, Deutsche Bank AG | Germany |
| BROUSSEAU | Eric | Professeur, Université de Paris 1 | France |
| CADBURY | Adrian | Former Chairman Cadbury-Schweppes and the Commission on Financial Aspects of Corporate Governance | United Kingdom |
| de CARMOY | Hervé | Président du Conseil d'Administration, Banque Industrielle et Mobilière Privée | France |

| Surname | First name | Affiliation | Country |
|---|---|---|---|
| CARTER | Alan | Senior Research Analyst, Andersen Consulting | United Kingdom |
| CELMER-HANSDORFER | Maria | Chief Expert, Ministry of Economy | Poland |
| CHARKHAM | Jonathan | Director, Great Universal Store | United Kingdom |
| CHARLETY | Patricia | Professeur, ESSEC | France |
| CHAVEZ-RUIZ | Javier | Dean of the Business School, ITAM, Mexico | Mexico |
| CHICOYE | Cécile | Ministère de l'Industrie, de la Poste et des Télécommunications | France |
| de COURCEL | Jérome | Responsable Tutelle, Animation, Finance, BNPI | France |
| de COURCEL | Whitney | Household | France |
| CRESPO | Fátima | Adviser, Directorate General for Industry, Ministry of Economy | Portugal |
| CSERNENSZKY | László | Head of Department, Ministry of Industry, Trade and Tourism | Hungary |
| DENHAM | Robert E. | CEO, Salomon Inc. | United States |
| DOLEJSI | Bohumil | Permanent Delegation to the OECD | Czech Republic |
| DOOMS | Ron | Directorate General for Industry, General Policy Co-ordination Department | Netherlands |
| ELMESKOV | Jorgen | Counsellor for Structural Policy, Economics Department, OECD | |
| ENDO | Hiroshi | Director, Economic Policy Bureau, Japan Federation of Economic Organisation | Japan |
| FEDDERSEN | Dieter | Feddersen, Laule, Scherzberg & Ohle Hansen Ewerwahn | Germany |

| Surname | First name | Affiliation | Country |
|---|---|---|---|
| FERM | Anders | Ambassador, Permanent Delegation to the OECD | Sweden |
| FOULT | Dominique | Chargée de Mission, Direction Générale des Etudes, Banque de France | France |
| FREDERICK | Richard | Administrator, Privatisation Unit and Private Sector Development, Directorate for Financial, Fiscal and Enterprise Affairs, OECD | |
| FREI | William | Deputy Head of Delegation, Permanent Delegation to the OECD | Switzerland |
| GALEY-LERUSTE | Sophie | Sous-Directeur, Ministère de l'Industrie, de la Poste et des Télécommunications | France |
| GALLAGHER | Martin | Counsellor, Permanent Delegation to the OECD | Australia |
| GASSMANN | Hans-Peter | Head, Industry Division, Directorate for Science, Technology and Industry, OECD | |
| GAVED | Matthew | Institute of Management, London School of Economics | United Kingdom |
| GERNANDT | Johan | Member of the Governing Board of the Swedish Central Bank | Sweden |
| GÖNENÇ | Rauf | Principal Administrator, Directorate for Science, Technology and Industry, OECD | |
| GREGORY | Holly | Weil, Gotshal & Manges, LLP | United States |
| GUIGOU | Didier | Senior Vice-President, Finance Communication, Rhône-Poulenc | France |

| Surname | First name | Affiliation | Country |
|---|---|---|---|
| HAINS | Jacques | Director, Corporate Law Policy Directorate, Industry Canada | Canada |
| HAMPEL | Sir Ronald | Chairman, ICI, and Chairman, The Committee on Corporate Governance | United Kingdom |
| HARAOKA | Naoyuki | Permanent Delegation to the OECD | Japan |
| HARLEY | Ed | Economic Adviser, Department of Trade and Industry | United Kingdom |
| HARUTA | Hiroshi | Member of the Steering Committee, Corporate Governance Forum, Professor, Kokugakuin University | Japan |
| HASEGAWA | Kimitoshi | Managing Director, Dai-ichi Life Research Institute Inc. | Japan |
| HELLNER | Cecilia | Counsellor, Permanent Delegation to the OECD | Sweden |
| HERX | Gerd | Head of Division, Federal Ministry of Economics | Germany |
| HOLMGAARD | Pernille | Ministry of Finance | Denmark |
| HONDA | Keikichi | Chairman and Representative Director, Nihon Sun Microsystems K.K. | Japan |
| ILNICKA-LEMBAS | Aniela | Chief Expert, Ministry of Economy | Poland |
| ISAKSSON | Mats | Principal Administrator, Directorate for Science, Technology and Industry, OECD | |
| JOHNSTON | Donald J. | Secretary-General, OECD | |
| JOHNSTONE | Elizabeth | National Director, Consulting, Blake Dawson Waldron Solicitors | Australia |

| Surname | First name | Affiliation | Country |
|---|---|---|---|
| KAISANLAHTI | Timo | Counsellor, Ministry of Trade, Industry and Commerce | Finland |
| KANG | Gil-Sang | Economic Advisor, Permanent Delegation to the OECD | Korea |
| KAWAUCHI | Yoshitada | Co-Executive Director, Corporate Governance Forum | Japan |
| KELLEY | Martha | Permanent Delegation to the OECD | United States |
| KIM | Young-Yul | Associate Research Fellow, Korea Institute for Industrial Economics & Trade | Korea |
| KINOSHITA | Komei | Auditor, Yamaichi Securities Co. Ltd. | Japan |
| KIRIBUCHI | Toshihiro | Senior Corporate Advisor to the Board of Directors, OMRON Corp. | Japan |
| KOJIMA | Susumu | Supervisor, Corporate Communication Center, OMRON Corp. | Japan |
| KOMATSUBARA | Shigeki | OECD Business and Industry Advisory Committee (BIAC) | |
| KRISTIANSEN | Hans | Money and Finance Division, Policy Studies Branch, Economics Department, OECD | |
| KRISTIANSSON | Björn | Företagsjuridik Nord & Co. AB | Sweden |
| KUNZ | Heidi | Chief Financial Officer, ITT Industries | United States |
| LÅFTMAN | Lennart | Managing Director, Swedish National Pension Fund, 5$^{th}$ Board | Sweden |

| Surname | First name | Affiliation | Country |
|---|---|---|---|
| LAU | Gregory E. | Executive Director, Executive Compensation and Corporate Governance, General Motors Corporation | United States |
| LEAL | Soledad | Permanent Delegation to the OECD | Mexico |
| LEE | Soo-Mi | Vice-President, Legal Department, Salomon Inc. | United States |
| de LEMOS GODINHO | Jorge | Ambassador, Permanent Delegation to the OECD | Portugal |
| LEV | Baruch | Professor, New York University, Stern School of Business | United States |
| LIOUKAS | Spyros | Ambassador, Permanent Delegation to the OECD | Greece |
| MACAK | Oldrich | Ministry of Trade and Industry | Czech Republic |
| MACDONALD | Nigel C.L. | Partner, Ernst & Young | United Kingdom |
| MAGNE | Yves | Ministère de l'Industrie, de la Poste et des Télécommunications | France |
| MAURY | Jean-Pierre | Chef de Bureau, Ministère de l'Industrie, de la Poste et des Télécommunications | France |
| METELO | Manuel | Adviser, Studies and Planning Office, Ministry of Economy | Portugal |
| MICHALSKI | Wolfgang | Director, Advisory Unit on Multi-disciplinary Issues, OECD | |
| MILES | Glenn A. | Corporate Governance Officer, CalPERS | United States |
| MILLSTEIN | Ira M. | Senior Partner, Weil, Gotshal & Manges, LLP | United States |

| Surname | First name | Affiliation | Country |
|---|---|---|---|
| MINAGAWA | Yasuhira | General Manager, Corporate Communication Center, OMRON Corp. | Japan |
| MIURA | Shozo | Président Directeur Général, Yamaichi France S.A. | Japan |
| MONKS | Robert A.G. | Principal, LENS | United States |
| MORITA | Kentaro | Industrial Structure Division, Industrial Policy Bureau, Ministry of International Trade and Industry | Japan |
| MOUY | Nadine | Bureau de l'Industrie, Ministère des Finances | France |
| MULDER | Ugur | European Commission, DG XII | |
| NEUBAUER | Friedrich | Professor, International Institute for Management Development (IMD) | Switzerland |
| NEZU | Risaburo | Director, Directorate for Science, Technology and Industry, OECD | |
| NORD | Gunnar | Director, Corporate Governance Forum | Sweden |
| OGINO | Hiroshi | Member of the Steering Committee, Corporate Governance Forum | Japan |
| OHLSSON | Robert | Företagsjuridik Nord & Co. AB | Sweden |
| de PANAFIEU | Guy | Vice-Président, Lyonnaise des Eaux | France |
| PAPACONSTANTINOU | Georges | Principal Administrator, Economic Analysis and Statistics Division, Directorate for Science, Technology and Industry, OECD | |

| Surname | First name | Affiliation | Country |
|---------|-----------|-------------|---------|
| PARK | Young-Ki | Counsellor, Permanent Delegation to the OECD | Korea |
| PASTRE | Olivier | Directeur Général, GP Banque | France |
| PEBEREAU | Michel | Président Directeur Général, Banque Nationale de Paris | France |
| PERETSMAN | Nancy B. | Managing Director, Allen & Company Inc. | United States |
| PEZZINI | Mario | Head of Division, Territoral Development Service, OECD | |
| POTMA | Harry | Ministry of Economic Affairs | Netherlands |
| PULQUERIO de CASTRO | Armando | Counsellor, Permanent Delegation to the OECD | Portugal |
| RALETICH-FAJICIC | Maria | Counsellor, Permanent Delegation to the OECD | Canada |
| RICE III | Joseph L. | Chairman and Chief Executive Officer, Clayton, Dubilier & Rice Inc. | United States |
| RIFFLET | Luc | Counsellor, Permanent Delegation to the OECD | Belgium |
| ROSS GOOBEY | Alastair | Chief Executive Officer, Hermes | United Kingdom |
| SAGNAC | Claudie | Ministère de l'Industrie, de la Poste et des Télécommunications | France |
| SAINT-GEOURS | Jean | Ancien Président, Commission des Opérations de Bourse | France |
| SAKUMA | Kyoko | Japanese Embassy, Vienna | Japan |
| SALESSE | Robert | Ministère de l'Industrie, de la Poste et des Télécommunications | France |
| SAUTTER | Christian | Inspecteur Général des Finances | France |

| Surname | First name | Affiliation | Country |
|---|---|---|---|
| SCHULTE-NOELLE | Henning | Chairman of the Board of Management, Allianz AG | Germany |
| de SELLIERS | Guy | Deputy Vice President, European Bank for Reconstruction and Development | |
| SERRELIS | Dimitris | Secretary, Permanent Delegation to the OECD | Greece |
| SHELTON | Joanna R. | Deputy Secretary-General, OECD | |
| SIMPSON | Anne | Joint Managing Director, PIRC Ltd | United Kingdom |
| SKOG | Rolf | Director, Swedish Corporate Governance Forum | Sweden |
| SONG | Wong-Soon | General Councel, Samsung Group | Korea |
| STÅLHAND | Johan | General Counsel, Skandinaviska Enskilda Banken | Sweden |
| SUNDE | Bent F. | Assistant Director General, Ministry of Trade and Industry | Norway |
| TATEISI | Nobuo | Chairman, OMRON Corporation | Japan |
| TEGNER | Per | Deputy Under-Secretary, Ministry of Industry and Commerce | Sweden |
| VALASKAKIS | Kimon | Ambassador, Permanent Delegation to the OECD | Canada |
| VERLAETEN | M-P | Adviser, Ministry of Economic Affairs | Belgium |
| VURGUN | Kudret | Director, Istanbul Stock Exchange, Listing Department | Turkey |

| Surname | First name | Affiliation | Country |
|---|---|---|---|
| WEINBACH | Lawrence | Chairman and Chief Executive Officer, Andersen Worldwide | United States |
| WOLTER | Stefan | Chef du Service Economique, Office Fédéral de l'industrie, des arts et métiers et du travail | Switzerland |
| WOO | Tae-Hee | Director, Industrial Policy Division, Ministry of Trade, Industry and Energy | Korea |
| WORMS | Gérard | Président du Conseil des Commanditaires, Banque Rothschild et Compagnie Banque Paris | France |
| WUNDERLIN | Bernhard | Managing Director, Harald Quandt Holding GmbH | Germany |
| YANAI | Hiroyuki | Co-Executive Director, Corporate Government Forum, Japan | Japan |
| YOSHIDA | Yasuo | Chief Representative, The Dai-ichi Mutual Life | Japan |
| ZEHNDER | Jean-Pierre | Ambassador, Permanent Delegation to the OECD | Switzerland |

## ANNEX 2

## PARTIAL LISTING OF CORPORATE GOVERNANCE GUIDELINES AND CODES OF "BEST PRACTICE"

### Australia

- Working Group representing Australian Institute for Company Directors, Australian Society of Certified Practicing Accountants, Business Council of Australia, Law Council of Australia, The Institute of Chartered Accountants in Australia and The Securities Institute of Australia, *Corporate Practices and Conduct* (Bosch Report) (3rd ed., 1995).

- Australian Investment Managers Association, *A Guide for Investment Managers and A Statement of Recommended Corporate Practice* (June 1995).

### Belgium

- *Report of the Belgian Commission on Corporate Governance* (Brussels Stock Exchange) (Cardon Report) (1998).

- Federation of Belgian Companies, *Corporate Governance Principles* (1998).

### Brazil

- Brazilian Institute of Corporate Directors, *Brazilian Code of Best Practices* (Preliminary Proposal, April 1997).

### Canada

- Toronto Stock Exchange Committee on Corporate Governance in Canada, *"Where Were the Directors?" Guidelines for Improved Corporate Governance in Canada* (Dey Report) (December 1994).

**France**

- Conseil National du Patronat Français (CNPF) and Association Française des Entreprises Privées (AFEP), *The Boards of Directors of Listed Companies in France* (Viénot Report) (10 July 1995).

**Hong Kong**

- The Stock Exchange of Hong Kong, *Code of Best Practice* (December 1989; revised June 1996).

**India**

- Confederation of Indian Industry, *Desirable Corporate Governance in India – A Code* (Draft, 19 April 1997).

**Ireland**

- Irish Association of Investment Managers, *Statement of Best Practice on the Role and Responsibilities of Directors of Public Limited Companies* (1991; revised 1993).

**Japan**

- Japan Federation of Economic Organizations (Keidanren), *Urgent Recommendations Concerning Corporate Governance* (Provisional Draft, 16 September 1997).

- Corporate Governance Forum of Japan, *Corporate Governance Principles – A Japanese View* (Interim Report, 30 October 1997).

**Kyrgyz Republic**

- Working Group on Corporate Governance, *Handbook on Best Practice Corporate Governance in the Kyrgyz Republic* (Draft, June 1997).

**Netherlands**

- Committee on Corporate Governance, *Corporate Governance in the Netherlands – Forty Recommendations* (Peters Report) (25 June 1997).

**South Africa**

- The Institute of Directors in Southern Africa, *The King Report on Corporate Governance* (King Report) (29 November 1994).

**United Kingdom**

- *Report of the Committee on the Financial Aspects of Corporate Governance* (Cadbury Report) (1 December 1992).

- *Committee on Corporate Governance Final Report* (Hampel Report) (January 1998).

**United States**

- The American Law Institute, *Principles of Corporate Governance: Analysis and Recommendations* (1992).

- American Bar Association Section of Business Law, *Corporate Directors Guidebook* (1978; revised 1994).

- General Motors Board of Directors, *GM Board of Directors Corporate Governance Guidelines on Significant Corporate Governance Issues* (January 1994; revised August 1995; revised June 1997).

- National Association of Corporate Directors, *Report of the NACD Commission on Director Professionalism* (November 1996).

- Teachers Insurance and Annuity Association – College Retirement Equities Fund (TIAA-CREF), *TIAA-CREF on Corporate Governance* (1996).

- California Public Employees' Retirement System (CalPERS), *Corporate Governance Coret Principles & Guidelines* (Draft, March 1998).

- The Business Roundtable, *Statement on Corporate Governance* (September 1997).

OECD PUBLICATIONS, 2, rue André-Pascal, 75775 PARIS CEDEX 16
PRINTED IN FRANCE
(92 98 04 1) ISBN 92-64-16056-6 – No. 49993 1998